God Speaks Tenderly

MARIE SHROPSHIRE

HARVEST HOUSE PUBLISHERS
Eugene, Oregon 97402

GOD SPEAKS TENDERLY
Copyright © 1997 by Marie Shropshire
Published by Harvest House Publishers
Eugene, Oregon 97402

Library of Congress Cataloging-in-Publication Data

Shropshire, Marie, 1921–
    God speaks tenderly / Marie Shropshire.
            p.   cm.
        ISBN 1-56507-693-1
        1. Consolation.   I. Title.
    BV4905.2.S487   1997
    242—dc20   97-9004
                                                                CIP

97 98 99 00 01 02 / BP / 10 9 8 7 6 5 4 3 2 1

Contents

Perfect Through Christ

The LORD redeems his servants; no one will be condemned who takes refuge in him (Psalm 34:22).

*H*ave you ever approached your devotional time with a feeling of guilt and unworthiness? If you have trusted Jesus as your Savior, you need never feel reluctant about coming to Him in complete confidence. You can come in His name. He will accept you. If you have sinned, ask His forgiveness and be assured of His pardon. Regardless of what you have done or failed to do, you can take refuge in Him. He speaks tenderly and forgives you. Paul assures us, "there is now no condemnation for those who are in Christ Jesus" (Romans 8:1).

We are accepted by God not on the basis of performance but on the basis of the blood of Jesus shed on our behalf. We do not earn our salvation by our good works. It is a free gift of God because of His love and grace. All that is required is repentance. The atoning sacrifice of Christ is sufficient and complete. We are not under law but grace.

Our repentance and trust in Christ have gained our position in Him. A new spiritual life has been imparted to us. We can rest in that assurance. We can enter His presence—not with fear or feelings of condemnation but with joy. He is our eternal refuge. He declares we are His beloved children.

God never expects us to be perfect in ourselves. We are perfect only through Christ. When the Word tells us to be perfect, it means we are to be spiritually mature. We grow in spiritual maturity as we live daily in the presence of Christ.

God's Everlasting Presence

Never will I leave you; never will I forsake you (Hebrews 13:5).

*T*imes come to all of us when we especially need to be reminded of God's promise never to leave us or forsake us. Trials are the common lot of all who choose to follow Jesus. At such times, we may wonder if God has forsaken us. But He has declared that He never will. We can depend on His promises; God cannot lie. He is true to Himself and to us in every situation and at all times.

We may experience discouragement, defeat, or failure. God seems far away. But He has not left us. He knows what we're going through, and we can be sure He will bring us out. We may have to wait longer than we want to, but deliverance will come—in God's way and in His timing. He always knows what is best for us.

When we renew our minds daily by reading the Word of God and putting it into practice, we will find that His will is good—and only good. We draw strength and are assured of God's everlasting presence as we spend quiet time in His Word—meditating on it and talking to God. When things go contrary to what we believe is best, our emotions may tell us God has abandoned us, but He hasn't. He is *always* present to help us and encourage us.

Fredrick W. Faber, a nineteenth-century poet, expressed his thoughts about God's seeming absence in these words:

> He hides Himself so wondrously
>   As though there were no God;
> He is least seen when all the powers
>   Of ill are most abroad.
> Or He deserts us at the hour
>   The fight is almost lost.
> And seems to leave us to ourselves
>   Just when we need Him most.
> It is not so, but so it looks;

And we lose courage then;
And doubts will come if God hath kept
His promise to men.

Regardless of what comes and regardless of our feelings, we can rest assured that God will never leave us or forsake us.

Cry Out to God

*The eyes of the LORD are on the righteous
and his ears are attentive to their cry*
(Psalm 34:15).

When unfortunate circumstances come our
way, we sometimes wonder if God has taken
His eyes off us and no longer hears our cry for help.
But His promise is sure. His eyes are always on
those who are righteous through His Son.

Peter reminds us that "in [God's] great mercy he
has given us new birth into a living hope" (1 Peter
1:3). This "living hope" energizes our spirits and
helps us to look on the bright side of life, knowing
that God will work things out for our good.

The eyes of the Lord are upon us—not to check
up on us to see how well we are performing, as
some of us were taught, but to come to our aid.

Knowing that God cares about everything that concerns us, let's put away every thought that would disturb our minds and rest in His goodness and love.

We are free to follow Peter's counsel: "Casting the whole of your care [all your anxieties, all your worries, all your concerns, once and for all] on Him, for He cares for you affectionately and cares about you watchfully" (1 Peter 5:7 AMP).

God is not the initiator of our troubles, but when they come He is able to turn them to good. Dr. Charles Stanley said, "When trouble comes, He masterfully takes it and shapes it into an instrument of eternal purpose." Nothing can stop God's plan and purpose.

Regardless of what we face, God is committed to giving us the strength to get through it. "For the eyes of the LORD range throughout the earth to strengthen those whose hearts are fully committed to him" (2 Chronicles 16:9).

Clothed with Joy

My soul faints with longing for your salvation, but I have put my hope in your word. My eyes fail, looking for your promise (Psalm 119:81,82).

Most of us occasionally experience times when we feel as David did when he wrote the above words. We keep hoping for deliverance from whatever our trial may be, but our hope seems in vain. We have put our hope in God's Word—why doesn't He answer?

Let's remember that God is at work in our circumstances even when we see no evidence of His hand. Knowing that God is moving on our behalf, we need not give in to despondency. Our hope is in God, and He will never let us down.

On the cross, Jesus experienced intense physical

pain—but His physical suffering did not compare with His emotional suffering. His feelings of despair were much more real than yours and mine.

In our times of despair, we know that Jesus has been there. He understands completely. We need not bottle up our feelings. We can express them freely to the One who understands and cares.

David's despair did not drive him to self-pity, as you and I may be prone to allow. It drove him to the arms of God. There he found rest until his tempest had passed. On one occasion, David wrote, "You turned my wailing into dancing; you removed my sackcloth and clothed me with joy" (Psalm 30:11).

Most often our wailing will not be turned to joy as soon as we'd like. But if we continue looking to God, He will intervene in our behalf. "If our hearts hunger for Him," says author Dr. Dan Allender, "then despair is our ally, our friend, our guide, opening our hearts to the bright hope of seeing His face."

Then we will know that our hope in His Word has not been in vain.

The Spark of Hope

A righteous man may have many troubles,
but the LORD delivers him from them all
(Psalm 34:19).

A friend asked me, "Since we are Christians and
following Christ the best we know how, why
do we have so many troubles?" God never promised
us a trouble-free life—but He does promise to deliver us from our troubles. Trouble may be the fire
God uses to refine us and to fashion us into the
saints He created us to be.

None of us enjoys or appreciates trouble. But
often, after the troublesome situation has passed, we
recognize that God was in it. In the end, He turns it
into good for us and for His glory.

In our down times we can rekindle the spark of
hope that God has placed deep within our hearts.

The flame flickers low when trouble strikes. We may feel that the fire of hope has died completely. We *can* fan the flame to life again. Hoping in God and His Word will revive the flame.

We need never allow trouble to destroy our hope in God. He is the God of hope. Paul wrote to the Romans, "May the God of hope fill you with all joy and peace as you trust in him, so that you may overflow with hope by the power of the Holy Spirit" (Romans 15:13).

The psalmist declared, "We wait in hope for the LORD; he is our help and our shield" (Psalm 33:20). We, too, can wait in hope, knowing that God has not forgotten us or left us alone in our distress. The world's darkness cannot engulf us when we remember that God has delivered us from darkness and transferred us into His marvelous light.

All that the Lord was to the psalmist, He will be to you and me. When we put our hope in the Lord, we will not be disappointed. We can never be sure that troubles won't come, but we can be sure of God's unfailing presence.

The Wilderness Requirement

For the LORD is good and his love endures forever; his faithfulness continues through all generations (Psalm 100:5).

*O*ur wilderness experiences sometimes cause us to temporarily wonder about God's goodness and faithfulness. Our human nature may rise above our spiritual selves. We wish we could bypass the wilderness. "To bypass the wilderness in our journey to the Promised Land is to bypass God," said minister and author Jamie Buckingham. God has a purpose for every spiritual wilderness He leads us through. Our consolation is that *He is leading us*. We never tread our spiritual journey alone.

We would like to arrive at our heavenly destination without having to go through storms or wilderness experiences. But such circumstances are a requirement for developing a mature Christian life.

We may look at certain individuals and their accomplishments and think their lives have always been easy. But if we could get to know them, we probably would find that their lives have been one wilderness experience after another. Do you know of any "great" men or women who have not gone through the wilderness of doubt, fear, or discouragement? I don't. How did they do it? *They knew the faithfulness of God and relied on Him.*

We remember David as a great king of Israel. But what trials he had to go through to become all he became! The psalms he wrote are an encouragement to us because we can identify with them. Many of David's psalms were written while he was in the midst of a wilderness experience filled with conflicts. But David always concluded that the "Lord is good and his love endures forever" (Psalm 100:5).

The same God who revealed His love and faithfulness to David is our God. He loves us as much as He loved David. God guided David through his wilderness experiences, and He will do the same for you and me.

God Is with Us!

*As I was with Moses, so I will be
with you. . . . Be strong and courageous*
(Joshua 1:5,6).

The above words were spoken by the Lord to
Joshua after Moses died. Moses had faithfully
led the Israelites out of the land of Egypt. Now it
was time for Joshua to take over. Trying to fill the
shoes of such a great leader must have been over-
whelming. Besides missing his close friend, Joshua
surely felt inadequate for the task ahead.

You and I may not be called on to finish the
work someone else has begun. We may not be overwhelmed by a task we've been asked to assume.
But we all experience times when we need to hear
the words the Lord spoke to Joshua.

What enabled the early believers to get through their tempestuous times was their faith in God and His unfailing Word. Many times that was *all* they had to help them combat discouragement. The same may often be true for you and me. But that is all we need. We can be sure that whatever our situation, the Lord will come through for us. We can be victorious through Him.

When we stop striving and trying to do things apart from God, God will intervene in our behalf. As we look to Him, He will bring encouragement to our hearts.

Trials can be steppingstones to greater faith in God. Through them, we may obtain a greater measure of God's grace toward us. Difficult as it may be, we can look upon our trials as opportunities for spiritual growth.

The Lord tells us "in quietness and trust is your strength" (Isaiah 30:15). When I became fearful as a young child, I knew if Mother or Daddy were near I need not be afraid. They would protect me. So it is with our heavenly Father. He is always near to absorb our fears and give us courage. As He was with Moses and Joshua, He is with us.

Promised Blessings

*I will never stop doing good to them. . . .
I will rejoice in doing them good* (Jeremiah
32:40,41).

The above promise was spoken by the Lord to
His people through His prophet Jeremiah. Do
we realize those wonderful words apply to us too?
You may feel that God isn't doing you good in your
present circumstances—most of us go through such
times of doubt.

But God works through our circumstances to
bring us to a place of knowing His pleasure in blessing us. Having no other place to turn, we turn to
the Lord and find Him more than sufficient to meet
every need. Peter tells us, "His divine power has
given us everything we need for life and godliness
through our knowledge of him" (2 Peter 1:3).

I wondered for a long time why I wasn't experiencing some of God's promised blessings. Then I noticed that the Scripture says it's "through our knowledge of him" that He has given us these things. One of God's greatest desires is that we have an intimate knowledge of Him. The better we know Him, the more we are able to receive His intended blessings.

"[God] is rejoicing over my good with all his heart and with all his soul," says John Piper. "He virtually breaks forth into song when he hits upon a new way to do me good." This truth is confirmed in what Moses told the Israelites centuries ago: "All these blessings will come upon you and accompany you if you obey the LORD your God" (Deuteronomy 28:2). Then he enumerated the blessings the Lord had stored up for them if they obeyed Him.

The psalmist David wrote, "Delight yourself in the LORD and he will give you the desires of your heart" (Psalm 37:4). One of my desires, as is yours, is to have the Lord "do me good" as He told Jeremiah He would. David says the answer is to delight ourselves in the Lord. "Draw from the well," says Lloyd Ogilvie, "for the more you draw the more the artesian replenishment of the Spirit will be given."

The Lord Comforts

I, even I, am he who comforts you
(Isaiah 51:12).

S everal years ago, I experienced a trying time in
my life and found great consolation in the above
Scripture and similar verses. I've found that regardless of what I'm going through, the Lord is present
to comfort me.

Even in the unlikely book of Job, I found an
assuring verse: "Now acquaint yourself with Him,
and be at peace; thereby good will come to you"
(Job 22:21 NKJV). As we acquaint ourselves more and
more with God, we find His grace and peace to be
more than sufficient. He can keep us strong regardless of what happens. God is able to free us from
hurts of our past and our present.

"When God's Word really becomes a part of your inner life, you have something upon which to base your life," says pastor Morris Sheats. "No longer can fear beat you into the ground when a problem arises. You have confidence because of God's Word."

The Lord wants to bring us to a place of knowing Him so well that we feel His comfort and peace when there seems to be no reason for it. When we feel weighted down by the anxieties of life, the Lord can lift us up and give us unspeakable comfort. To give comfort is one of the Lord's wonderful ministries to us.

Many things that happen to us are simply the result of living in this world. We have a choice of allowing unpleasant happenings to make us bitter or better. If Jesus lives in us, our old life is finished and our new life is complete in Him. We can accept the comfort He offers.

Meditations of the Heart

Oh, how I love your law! I meditate on it all day long (Psalm 119:97).

*T*he psalmist realized that knowledge alone does not promote spiritual growth. That's one reason he meditated on the Word all day. Most of us can grab snatches of time throughout the day to recall a Scripture verse and let it linger a moment in our minds. To pray or meditate unceasingly means not to give up.

Meditation on the Word brings peace, provides personal growth, rebuilds our thought life, and gives guidance and direction to our lives.

Peter tells us, "As newborn babes, desire the pure milk of the word, that you may grow thereby"

(1 Peter 2:2 NKJV). To "desire the pure milk of the word" is to go beyond reading and understanding with the natural senses. It means to hear with our spiritual ears and see with our spiritual eyes.

It is largely through meditation that the Holy Spirit guides us. He speaks to us in His quiet voice to give us direction. One of my friends, now with the Lord, said she most often heard God's voice while washing dishes. She spent hours every day reading her Bible. With her mind saturated with the Word, she was able to hear God speak while she performed menial tasks.

When the Israelites left Egypt, the Lord wanted to free them of their old mind-set. He emphasized the importance of their giving attention to His principles. I was impressed as I read the book of Deuteronomy that the Lord said over and over, "so that it may go well with you." The Lord sincerely desires that things in our lives go well for us.

There is so much in the world to keep our minds earth-bound. I must be selective in what I give my time and attention to. So almost every morning I pray one of the psalmist's prayers: "May the words of my mouth and the meditation of my heart be pleasing in your sight, O LORD, my Rock and my Redeemer" (Psalm 19:14).

Living in God's Kingdom

For he has rescued us from the dominion of darkness and brought us into the kingdom of the Son he loves (Colossians 1:13).

I'm sure I had read the above verse dozens of times, but one day I read it with fresh insight. Tears of gratitude filled my eyes as I meditated on the meaning. Before we accepted Christ as Savior, we lived in the dominion of spiritual darkness. But because of God's great love for us, He rescued us and brought us into His kingdom. Now, even though we live in the world, we are citizens of the heavenly kingdom.

We don't have to live on the fringe of God's highest. His perfect will for us is peace and joy. He purchased that for us at Calvary. We no longer need to react out of our emotions, living according to whatever befalls us. We can now live in the knowledge of the resurrected Lord within us. Our smiles are no longer on the outside only but are produced from the genuine joy originating from deep within our hearts.

Jesus said, "The kingdom of God is within you" (Luke 17:21). Paul defines the kingdom of God as a kingdom "of righteousness, peace and joy in the Holy Spirit" (Romans 14:17). If I'm lacking in peace and joy, I need to examine myself and see if I've forgotten I'm a member of God's eternal kingdom.

God wants to give us spiritual insight into His kingdom and what it means to live there—here and now. It was in order to satisfy His great love for us that God gave His perfect Son to suffer and die for us. In so doing, He opened the way for us to become His very own beloved children.

While we wait for the work to be completed in us, we need to be gentle with ourselves just as God is. Whether we always feel like it or not, we *have* been rescued from the kingdom of darkness and transferred into the kingdom of light.

God's Love Revealed Through Adversity

My soul finds rest in God alone; my salvation comes from him (Psalm 62:1).

*T*he psalmist David experienced times when he knew for certain that God was His only source of rest and salvation. On one occasion he said, "From my youth I have been afflicted and close to death; I have suffered your terrors and am in despair" (Psalm 88:15). And, amazingly, he also said, "It was good for me to be afflicted so that I might learn your decrees" (Psalm 119:71).

God permits trials in our lives. He reveals His power and love through them.

George Mueller, widely known as a man of faith, said, "Difficulties, limitations, hindrances . . . are

the very agencies God uses to cause us to grow."
Someone once said that Mueller's faith came to
fruition through trials, obstacles, difficulties, and
defeats—all of which God *affectionately* placed in
life's pathway.

It seems strange to us that anyone would use the
term "affectionately" to describe God's placing trials
in someone's life. But Mueller knew that trials
caused him to realize his dependence on God.

The Lord never allows anything to come against
us that we cannot bear. The old hymn "How Firm
a Foundation" says, "The sun shall not smite thee;
I only design thy dross to consume and thy gold
to refine."

Protected from the Storm

Do not be terrified; do not be discouraged, for the LORD your God will be with you wherever you go (Joshua 1:9).

These words spoken to Joshua by the Lord are also for you and me. God's desire is that we be so vitally united to Him that we know his presence and, whatever we face, we will not be terrified. Regardless of how long we've known the Lord as Savior, we still face times when we want to ask, "But Lord, what about this?"

We can be assured that every problem and situation is an opportunity for God to manifest His power in our behalf. He wants us to look through the problem to Him. We need to train ourselves to look for His presence and power in *every* circumstance. We can learn to see our problems as blessings in disguise. David reminds us, "He who dwells in the shelter of the Most High will rest in the shadow of the Almighty" (Psalm 91:1).

Hannah Whitall Smith said, "The comfort or discomfort of our inner life depends upon the dwelling place of our souls, just as the comfort or discomfort of our outward life depends largely upon the dwelling place of our bodies." For instance, I can stand inside my house and watch a rainstorm. It doesn't touch me; I am protected. I can also stand in my *spiritual* dwelling place and watch a storm in my life and remain unharmed.

We find our surety *in* Jesus, not in knowing about Him. Faith about Him is not sufficient to carry us through times when we feel terrified of the circumstances around us. Only in His presence and by His grace will we find strength to stand. Basking in His love, we find endurance and courage.

When our situation seems hopeless, we can remember that nothing is impossible with God. One of my friends said, "I'm trying to keep my eyes on God, but it's hard when life is so difficult." God knows that. That's why He keeps reminding us of His sufficiency. He really *is* with us.

Faith Overcomes All

This is the victory that has overcome the world, even our faith (1 John 5:4).

Today, as never before, you and I need a vital faith in a supernatural God. Mere human strength will not sustain us in the hours ahead. I receive letters from friends who feel their situation is hopeless. One friend wrote, "I don't understand why all this is happening to me." I reminded her that Jesus said, "In this world you will have trouble. But take heart! I have overcome the world" (John 16:33).

God is bringing us to a place of dependence on Him. Mere theology won't suffice. We must have reliable answers from the living Word. God's Word was never meant to be mere doctrine or theory. His Word is down-to-earth and applicable to every situation we face in our very real world. It is a guide to daily living.

God is so practical and so compassionate that He even included in His Word humane laws such as the command not to take a mother bird from her nest (Deuteronomy 22:6). If God is that interested in His little creatures, how much more does He care about everything that concerns you and me?

God gives us faith to trust Him just as He gives grace. We do nothing to earn either grace or faith. However, Paul tells us that "faith comes from hearing the message, and the message is heard through the word of Christ" (Romans 10:17). Hearing the Word imparts faith. Our faith is developed as we feed on the Word and meditate on it.

Faith is not a feeling. We are able to exercise faith because it is supported by God's Word. It is God's purpose to use every circumstance of our lives to bring us to greater maturity and greater faith in Him. The writer to the Hebrews said, "Let us draw near to God with a sincere heart in full assurance of faith. . . . Let us hold unswervingly to the hope we profess, for he who promised is faithful" (Hebrews 10:22,23).

We *will* to believe regardless of circumstances and our feelings. We know that "he who has promised is faithful." The better we know Him, the more assurance we have of His faithfulness.

When the Israelites had settled in Canaan, Joshua reminded them, "You know with all your heart and soul that not one of all the good promises the LORD your God gave you has failed. Every promise has been fulfilled; not one has failed" (Joshua 23:14).

You and I can remind ourselves that not one of God's promises to us has failed. God is as faithful as His promises. He gives us the amazing promise that our faith overcomes the world.

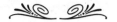

Turn On the Light!

Then you will know the truth, and the truth will set you free. . . . So if the Son sets you free, you will be free indeed (John 8:32,36).

*T*he grace of God frees us not only from the curse of the law, it also frees us from having to accomplish and perform certain acts in order to be acceptable to God. He invites us to be the unique persons He created each of us to be.

Before Jesus came, people were bound by the law. The purpose of the law was to show us our utter helplessness to save ourselves. Paul reminded the Galatians, "A man is not justified by observing the law, but by faith in Jesus Christ" (Galatians 2:16).

If we have trusted Christ as Savior, we belong
to Him and need no longer feel condemned. Paul
expressed it like this: "God made him who had no
sin to be sin for us, so that in him we might become
the righteousness of God" (2 Corinthians 5:21). Jesus
bore our sins for us, and now, as children of God, we
are righteous through Christ. We are free to enjoy
life as He lives His life through us.

Some time ago I received a phone call from a
friend loaded with false guilt. She had moved out
of her place of rest into a place of condemnation. The
adversary used the occasion to cause her to doubt
God's love for her. I reminded her that "God did not
send his Son into the world to condemn the world,
but to save the world through him" (John 3:17).

When we sin, the Holy Spirit brings conviction
so that we can repent, receive forgiveness, and become free. It is the enemy who condemns. God is
gentle; the enemy is tormenting.

Our relationship with God is never based on
how we feel. It's based on God's faithfulness. We
cannot separate ourselves from His love. We may
feel unworthy, but His grace is greater than all our
sins. The entrance of His light dispels darkness. We
don't have to struggle to drive out the darkness. All
we have to do is turn on the light.

The need for striving to "be" or to "do" can be laid aside. Christ has finished the work of salvation for us and invites us to rest in His completed work.

When life seems to tumble in on us, we sometimes feel like giving up. That's the time to remember that God is for us. Even when we're out of His will, we are still in His grace.

I find it really important to begin each day constructively. What we read or meditate on in those first few minutes of the day can influence our whole day. We can choose a verse of Scripture or other gem of truth to undergird us throughout the day. Then, in the midst of distractions, we can turn our attention back to the One who lives within us, the One who came to set us free.

In Harmony
with God

Do not be anxious about anything, but in everything, by prayer and petition, with thanksgiving, present your requests to God (Philippians 4:6).

*P*aul makes it clear to the Philippians (and to us) that we can choose not to be anxious or worried about anything. He adds that we are to make our requests to God with thanksgiving. The only way I can make my requests with thanksgiving is to know that my prayers are heard.

Sometimes, with our natural senses, we can see nothing to be thankful for. But when we realize that God invites us to come to Him with our problems and that He's interested in everything that concerns us, we take hope. The Word tells us, "We know that in all things God works for the good of those who love him, who have been called according to his purpose" (Romans 8:28).

God wants us to make *definite* requests, even though He already knows our needs and desires. Soon after Solomon became king of Israel, God appeared to him one night and said, "Ask for whatever you want me to give you" (2 Chronicles 1:7). Solomon asked for wisdom, and that is what God gave him—along with many other blessings. If our requests are vague or general, we probably won't know whether our prayers have been answered or not.

Prayer does not influence God's purposes, but it does influence His action. God's desires for us are always good, but He wants us to ask. James says, "You do not have, because you do not ask God" (James 4:2). God wants to hear from our lips a distinct expression of our desires. By making definite requests, we can test our desires to see if they are real and if they are in harmony with God's will. He wants us to know that if we ask according to His will, we will receive what we ask for.

One of the biggest obstacles to effective prayer is a feeling of guilt or unworthiness. If we feel that we have failed God, we may feel that we are not qualified to approach Him. Yet we know the Bible says that, if we confess our sins, God freely forgives us. Our sins may serve as powerful reminders of our need for a Savior and of our utter dependence on Him. Whatever our condition, God delights in our coming to Him with our needs and desires.

The writer to the Hebrews encourages us: "Let us then approach the throne of grace with confidence, so that we may receive mercy and find grace to help us in our time of need" (Hebrews 4:16). It's in our time of need that we are most encouraged to come. When we are anxious or worried, we are certainly experiencing a time of uncertainty. We don't ever have to be hesitant to come to the Lord with our concerns. He is more eager to answer than we are to ask.

Rejoice in the Lord!

I will rejoice in the LORD. . . . The Sovereign LORD is my strength; he makes my feet like the feet of a deer, he enables me to go on the heights (Habakkuk 3:18,19).

Habakkuk was in despair because of the decline of Judah. The leaders oppressed the poor and violence abounded. Habakkuk was perplexed and wondered why God didn't intervene and stop what looked inevitable. Times would be hard. Food would be scarce.

God assured Habakkuk that He would care for His own. God told him "the just shall live by his faith" (Habakkuk 2:4 KJV). When Habakkuk understood God's faithfulness, he knew he could rejoice in the Lord. He declared, "The Sovereign Lord is my strength." He knew God would make him as sure-footed as a deer, able to ascend to spiritual heights.

Our outlook may look as bleak as Habakkuk's, but as surely as God cared for Habakkuk, He will care for you and me. He asks only that we live by faith. The Lord is our strength regardless of what may be going on. Pressures may mount, circumstances may look unstable, our outlook may be grim, our hope for the future may be almost gone. But God knows. He will be our strength, our stability, and our hope.

The Lord especially delights in supplying our needs in times of chaos and confusion. "He gives strength to the weary and increases the power of the weak. Even youths grow tired and weary, and young men stumble and fall; but those who hope in the LORD will renew their strength. They will soar on wings like eagles; they will run and not grow weary, they will walk and not be faint" (Isaiah 40:29-31).

When our lives are invaded by trouble, we need not doubt God's presence or think He has abandoned us. Because of our trials, He can produce in us qualities that could not otherwise be. He is intimately involved in our lives and in everything that happens to us. It may be that He will use our trials to prepare us for greater service in His kingdom.

We can look confidently past our circumstances to Him.

Our reserve of spiritual and emotional energy may run low, but God's provision never runs low. It is always in plentiful supply. There is no darkness that God's light cannot penetrate. We need never allow despair to destroy our hopes or distract us from God and His loving care.

Others may make mistakes that affect us and governments may fail, but God never will. He will protect us and empower us to climb to spiritual heights with the sure-footedness of a deer.

We can sing with David: "The LORD is my rock, my fortress and my deliverer; my God is my rock, in whom I take refuge" (2 Samuel 22:2,3).

Receiving God's Grace

A man is not justified by observing the law, but by faith in Jesus Christ. So we, too, have put our faith in Christ Jesus that we may be justified by faith in Christ and not by observing the law, because by observing the law no one will be justified (Galatians 2:16).

*H*ow can we please God?" a conscientious young friend asked me. On one occasion the disciples asked Jesus a similar question. They asked, "'What must we do to do the works God requires?' Jesus answered, 'The work of God is this: to believe in the one he has sent'" (John 6:28,29).

Like my friend, the disciples thought there was something to do besides believing to be accepted by

God. The desire of the Father is that we believe Him and trust Him in every situation.

We are an achievement-oriented people. We seldom understand that Jesus invites us simply to rest in Him. Jesus said, "I am the vine; you are the branches. . . . Apart from me you can do nothing" (John 15:5). When we remain united to the Vine, we can trust Him to work through us without our having to sweat at trying to please Him.

The Galatian Christians also had problems believing that the gospel could be so simple. They thought they had to keep the law of Moses in order to be saved. Paul said to them, "You foolish Galatians! Who has bewitched you? . . . Christ was clearly portrayed as crucified. . . . Are you so foolish? After beginning with the Spirit, are you now trying to attain your goal by human effort?" (Galatians 3:1,3).

Christianity is not conforming to a list of rules and regulations. It's a matter of receiving God's grace. Christianity is a vital relationship with the Lord. It is living spontaneously, knowing we are united to Him.

After explaining the amazing gift of grace to the Romans, Paul said, "Shall we go on sinning so that grace may increase? By no means! We died to sin; how can we live in it any longer?" (Romans 6:1,2).

In our Christian growth, we experience, of course, periods of stumbling, just like babies learning to walk do. A baby's parents don't focus on the baby's falling but on his learning to walk. Likewise, God looks at our blunders and knows we are learning. He is a more loving, understanding parent than any human parent could ever be. God lifts us up without condemning us.

Whatever our position in life, whatever our level of growth, all our answers are found in God and His grace.

"Untouched by Trouble"

The fear of the LORD leads to life: Then one rests content, untouched by trouble (Proverbs 19:23).

*U*sually when the Bible speaks of the fear of the Lord, it means *reverence for* and *trust in* the Lord. That's what Solomon means in this verse. Complete and reverential trust in the Lord enables us to live "untouched by trouble." That doesn't mean we'll never experience trouble. No one can live in this fallen world without experiencing trouble. But we can be so aware of the Lord's presence that we don't allow troubles to consume us. We know God will lead us safely through them.

Solomon makes that clear in an earlier passage: "Have no fear of sudden disaster . . . for the LORD will be your confidence" (Proverbs 3:25,26). That is, the Lord will guide us through whatever comes. He is our refuge.

The psalmist David understood that truth. He said, "In you my soul takes refuge. I will take refuge in the shadow of your wings until the disaster has passed" (Psalm 57:1). David was no more exempt from the troubles of life than we are, but he knew he need not be afraid.

A woman I'll call "Jean" came to me intensely troubled because of her seeming inability to forgive a loved one who had hurt her deeply. "I want so much to forgive, but I just can't," she said. I felt somewhat helpless, but I led her in a prayer asking Jesus to be forgiveness in her.

The next day Jean called and excitedly exclaimed, "It worked! Jesus became forgiveness in me. All my hurt and bitterness are gone."

Regardless of the nature of our troubles, the Lord is present to heal us and give us support. He never forces Himself on us. He waits for us to ask for His help. He would like to spare us the pain, just as we often would like to spare our young-adult children pain. But we have to wait for them to ask for our counsel.

Sometimes, of course, the Lord knows we have to learn through experience. The millionaire R.G. LeTourneau could easily have paid for his four sons' college education, but he didn't. He required them to earn it for themselves. By so doing, he gave them something more valuable than money—stamina to stand on their own feet, looking to God rather than to their earthly father.

Our all-wise Father knows what we need and when we need it. His desire is for us to grow strong enough to withstand the troubles we're bound to face.

Blessed with Peace

May God himself, the God of peace, sanctify you through and through. May your whole spirit, soul and body be kept blameless at the coming of our Lord Jesus Christ (1 Thessalonians 5:23).

The Lord desires that we be sanctified, or set apart, to Him in spirit, soul, and body. Peter expressed similar counsel: "But grow in the grace and knowledge of our Lord and Savior Jesus Christ" (2 Peter 3:18). To be set apart to God and know His fullness, we must grow in our understanding of His love and grace.

It is also essential to understand the difference between our spirit and soul. The writer to the Hebrews says, "For the word of God . . . penetrates even to dividing soul and spirit, joints and marrow;

it judges the thoughts and attitudes of the heart" (Hebrews 4:12).

Someone once defined the soul as being "the point of union between body and spirit." Our bodies give us the use of our five senses whereby we contact the world in which we live. Our soul is the seat of our will, intellect, and emotions. A "soul" Christian is one who is controlled by his soul rather than by his spirit. If we follow our "soul" desires instead of following after the Spirit, we miss God's highest for us.

Paul says, "Offer yourselves to God, as those who have been brought from death to life; and offer the parts of your body to him as instruments of righteousness" (Romans 6:13). If I offer the parts of my body as instruments of righteousness, I'll guard my ears from listening to anything that dishonors God, I'll keep my tongue from speaking impure words, I'll keep my eyes from viewing anything unwholesome, I'll use my hands for creative purposes, and I'll use my mind to think only on holy things.

Too often we measure our spirituality only by what we *do*, but the Lord measures our spirituality by what we *are*. Above all else, He desires our devotion to Him and our complete obedience—which is always and only for our good.

53

A spiritual Christian is one whose soul and body are governed by his spirit, and whose spirit is in subjugation to the Holy Spirit. That is, his will, intellect, and emotions are regulated by the Holy Spirit. Paul says, "He who unites himself with the Lord is one with him in spirit" (1 Corinthians 6:17).

By accepting the death of Christ on the cross as our death, we lay aside anything contrary to Christ's will and give Him preeminence in our lives. Then the Spirit of the enthroned Christ flows into our lives. Regardless of where we are on our spiritual path, God loves us unconditionally and desires to bless us with His peace.

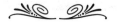

A Thirst for God

Like newborn babies, crave pure spiritual milk, so that by it you may grow up in your salvation (1 Peter 2:2).

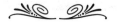

*O*ur salvation experience is only the beginning of our walk with the Lord. As surely as milk is necessary for the physical growth of a baby, the written Word of God is necessary for our spiritual growth. As a baby looks to his mother for food, you and I look to the Lord for our spiritual food. Through His written Word, God reveals Himself and His truth.

However, no one receives exactly the same understanding from the Word as another. We're not all on the same path. That is, our levels of growth are different, and we have different needs. In His personal love for us, God meets us where we are and speaks to us on our own level.

The path we're on at any given time determines the portion of truth we're able to understand. But it's our responsibility to make ourselves receptive to the truth God wants to reveal to us at any given time.

There are different levels of maturity. Often our difference in understanding stems from past experiences or from past teachings. Sometimes we have to unlearn some teachings which are not scriptural. It may be that our focus has been so narrow that we've missed some valuable truths. For several years, I read books published only by my denomination's publishing house. I didn't want anyone to rock my boat. Eventually I learned I was missing a lot of valuable insights.

No individual or denomination has the whole truth. We all need each other in order to be balanced. Christ, of course, is the *only* truth, and the Holy Spirit reveals Him to us through the Scriptures.

It might be said that the Bible contains *layers* of truth. One woman told me, "I read through the Bible once and I didn't know any more when I finished than when I started." Obviously her heart had not been prepared. When we have a thirst for God, layers of truth will be revealed.

Francis Bacon said, "There are three parts of truth: first, the inquiry, which is the wooing of it; secondly, the knowledge of it, which is the presence of it; and thirdly, the belief, which is the enjoyment of it." Bacon may not have been referring to the truth of the Bible, but his statement is applicable to scriptural truth.

The Lord is able to make His Word personal to us. Several years ago, I was invited to speak in a renowned church in Washington, D.C. The thought of it frightened me terribly. One morning the Lord made a certain Scripture real to me: "Do not be afraid; you will not suffer shame. Do not fear disgrace; you will not be humiliated" (Isaiah 54:4). His Word fed me and prepared me for what lay ahead. His Word will do the same for you.

God's Financial Provisions

Beloved, I pray that you may prosper in all things and be in health, just as your soul prospers (3 John 1:2 NKJV).

*A*ccording to John's words to his friend Gaius, when our souls are prospering—when we are giving God first place in our lives—we should also be prospering in other areas of life. Jesus said, "Seek first [God's] kingdom and his righteousness, and all these things will be given to you as well" (Matthew 6:33).

When the subject of money comes up, some people ask, "But what about Paul's words to Timothy? Doesn't he say money is a root of all evil?" No, not money—but the *love* of it may result in evil. He says, "For the love of money is a root of all kinds of evil" (1 Timothy 6:10). Love of money is *one* of the roots of evil.

God wants us to have a proper attitude toward money, using it wisely to bring glory to Him. Without money, how could the gospel be spread? How could the hungry be fed? Speaking through Malachi, God said, " 'Bring the whole tithe into the storehouse, that there may be food in my house. Test me in this,' says the LORD Almighty, 'and see if I will not throw open the floodgates of heaven and pour out so much blessing that you will not have room enough for it' " (Malachi 3:10).

I cannot explain why many people who tithe are lacking in some seeming necessities. It may have something to do with expectancy. If I were to withhold my tithe, I believe my greater sin would not be in failing to tithe, but in failing to trust God to make my income minus my tithe go as far as my entire income would have gone. God desires above all else that we *trust Him* in all things.

Paul told young Timothy, "Command those who are rich in this present world not to be arrogant nor to put their hope in wealth, which is so uncertain, but to put their hope in God, who richly provides us with everything for our enjoyment" (1 Timothy 6:17). Our trust is never to be in material wealth, but in God who supplies what we need.

When I began to study God's plan to bless His people financially, I came across this verse which encouraged me: "God is able to make all grace abound to you, so that in all things at all times, having all that you need, you will abound in every good work" (2 Corinthians 9:8).

The Bible gives many conditions for our being financially cared for. When I need instruction and encouragement in this area I read and meditate on verses such as: "Do not let this Book of the Law depart from your mouth; meditate on it day and night, so that you may be careful to do everything written in it. Then you will be prosperous and successful" (Joshua 1:8).

Valued by God

For God did not send his Son into the world to condemn the world, but to save the world through him (John 3:17).

*W*hen I was a girl we had a gray-and-white cat we called Tabby. Tabby lived outside and controlled any mice that might come into our barn. One day Tabby mysteriously disappeared. Several weeks later she returned badly injured. Her coat had been cruelly torn, exposing her bare flesh. We were especially saddened because Tabby was now afraid of us. Having been hurt, she dared not trust anyone for a while.

People who have been hurt are like that. Their wounded spirits are almost afraid to trust anyone. Yet on the inside they are crying out for someone they can trust, someone who cares. Having been hurt, these children of the King often see themselves as worthless and condemned.

In his prophecy, Isaiah makes it clear that Jesus came to heal the brokenhearted. "He has sent me to bind up the brokenhearted . . . to comfort all who mourn . . . to bestow on them a crown of beauty instead of ashes, the oil of gladness instead of mourning, and a garment of praise instead of a spirit of despair" (Isaiah 61:1-3).

Jesus was anointed by the Spirit to heal all who are crushed and overwhelmed with sorrows and cares, to deliver all who are in bondage to feelings of worthlessness. He came that we might exchange our heaviness for joy and our garments of despair for garments of praise.

Some of us sometimes feel like fragile reeds, so severely bruised that we are ready to be cast aside by the Father as worthless. But the Scripture says, "A bruised reed he will not break, and a smoldering wick he will not snuff out" (Isaiah 42:3).

Children playing along the banks of the Jordan River used reeds growing there to make musical pipes. As the pulp was hollowed out and holes bored through the outside, the pipes were often bruised in the making. The useless, bruised reed was thrown away. There were plenty more.

But when you and I are bruised in the making, Jesus never casts us off, saying there are plenty more without this one. The Lord specializes in mending reeds. We are valuable to Him.

"A smoldering wick he will not snuff out." When the oil in primitive lamps was used up, the wick burned dimly. It was quickly extinguished and replaced with a new wick and more oil was added. The compassion of Jesus never permits Him to extinguish a dimly burning wick. You and I may feel like dimly burning wicks, discouraged with ourselves. But the Lord is not discouraged with us. He will trim off our charred parts and make us useful. He sees us as valuable.

Choosing Abundant Life

I have set before you life and death,
blessings and curses. Now choose life . . .
(Deuteronomy 30:19).

The way we live our lives is largely a matter of choices. In many ways we choose our own destiny. That puts quite a responsibility on us. If it were not true, the Lord would not have said "choose life." Reading the above verse in context, we see that the Lord referred to choosing abundant life in contrast to living a lowly existence.

Abundant life does not result from doing certain things a certain way, having the right job, living in a certain place under the right circumstances, or knowing the right people. We must *choose* life. Just as surely as the Lord abundantly provided for those who made the choice to serve Him in the days of Abraham and Moses, He desires to bless those who make that choice today.

Jesus said, "I have come that they may have life, and have it to the full" (John 10:10). The Old Testament points toward Jesus, the giver of abundant life. Much of the New Testament describes the life He came to give and tells us how to obtain it. Near the end of the fourth gospel, John wrote, "These are written that you may believe that Jesus is the Christ, the Son of God, and that by believing you may have life in his name" (John 20:31).

John referred especially to eternal life, but that includes the abundant life that can be ours here and now. The four gospels are records of who Jesus is and what He came to accomplish in order that we might have life through Him. But we must *choose* to believe Him and His promises.

On one occasion God said to His people, "Oh, that their hearts would be inclined to fear me and keep all my commands always, so that it might go well with them . . . !" (Deuteronomy 5:29). God calls us His treasured possession. He longs to bless us, but we tie His hands when we fail to trust Him.

The psalmist declared, "Blessed is the man who fears the Lord, who finds great delight in his commands. . . . Wealth and riches are in his house, and his righteousness endures forever. . . . He will have no fear of bad news; his heart is steadfast, trusting in the LORD" (Psalm 112:1,3,7). The key to blessing is complete trust in the Lord. The choice is ours to make.

Even though we have been misunderstood or mistreated, or people and circumstances may have been unkind to us, our choices begin with our reactions. Although we may be tempted to retaliate, unforgiveness and bitterness cut us off from the life that is meant for us. When we love as Jesus loved, and trust the Father as He did, we choose the abundant life.

A Call to Trust

*When all kinds of trials and temptations
crowd into your lives, my brothers, don't re-
sent them as intruders, but welcome them
as friends! Realise that they come to test
your faith and to produce in you the qual-
ity of endurance. But let the process go
on until that endurance is fully developed,
and you will find that you have become
men of mature character with the right
sort of independence* (James 1:2-4 PHILLIPS).

*E*arly in life many of us thought that as long as
we walked with the Lord, everything would
fall into place just as we wanted it to. How contrary
to Scripture! Also, we couldn't appreciate light

without darkness. And, as James assures us, we couldn't grow in faith if we didn't have trials.

Disappointments and adverse circumstances show us where we are in our level of trust. Our security is in God, not in circumstances. We don't have to understand why things happen as they do. All we need to do is accept God's hand in our affairs and trust Him to work them out for our good. Charles Spurgeon said, "Many men owe the grandeur of their lives to their tremendous difficulties."

A look at the men of the Bible shows that their lives often didn't run smoothly. Joseph, who was mistreated by his brothers and sold into Egyptian slavery, must have wondered why his life went as it did. Later he saw the answer and said to his brothers, "You meant evil against me; but God meant it for good" (Genesis 50:20 NKJV).

When Paul was thrown into prison for preaching the gospel, he didn't ask why. He knew it was for the good of others. Paul wrote to his friends, "Now I want you to know, brothers, that what has happened to me has really served to advance the gospel. As a result, it has become clear throughout the whole palace guard and to everyone else that I am in chains for Christ" (Philippians 1:12,13).

In the same letter, Paul said, "I know what it is to be in need, and I know what it is to have plenty. I have learned the secret of being content in any and every situation, whether well fed or hungry, whether living in plenty or in want. I can do everything through him who gives me strength" (Philippians 4:12,13).

When we find ourselves struggling to get out of our present circumstances, maybe we should consider whether God is preparing us for something special. God is able to work out everything that happens to us for our good.

Carry Each
Other's Burdens

*Carry each other's burdens, and in this
way you will fulfill the law of Christ*
(Galatians 6:2).

L ife in Christ is meant to be a shared life. As
Christians, we are all members of the body of
Christ. Our lives touch each other and affect one another. Paul expressed it like this: "If one part suffers,
every part suffers with it; if one part is honored,
every part rejoices with it" (1 Corinthians 12:26).

We have the privilege of bearing one another's
burdens. Paul said, "We who are strong ought to
bear with the failings of the weak and not to please
ourselves" (Romans 15:1). All of us have strong
areas and weak areas. I can help you, and you can

help me. All of us are needy in one way or another. We never outgrow our need for each other.

We carry each other's burdens by praying for each other, fellowshipping together, and sharing our possessions when necessary. Another meaningful way we bear another's burdens is to make ourselves available to each other.

I would not be where I am today if a few committed Christian friends had not made themselves available to me. When I needed them several years ago as I went through a trying time, they were there. They supported me by showing me love and understanding, being with me when I needed them, listening to my feelings. Their constant prayers and continual words of encouragement helped me tremendously.

I read recently that the reason most people go to counselors is because they have failed to receive "appropriate love." We know that God is a God of love and "the God of all comfort" (2 Corinthians 1:3). He uses you and me to be channels of that love and comfort. When we feel at a loss for words, we can go to the burdened person as God's representative and simply *be with* him or her, letting our friend know we care.

The burdened person may need only to talk while we listen attentively. One day in an airport I happened to sit beside a young man who needed a listening ear. As he talked, pouring out his feelings of hurt, I knew little to say or do except to give an occasional sympathetic nod or offer a word of encouragement. After about an hour I heard a deep sigh and the words, "Whew! It feels good just to talk to someone who understands."

Before I could reply, he went on, "As soon as I saw you come through the door I knew you were a Christian. I could tell by the glow on your face." On that particular day I couldn't have felt less like being a burden-bearer, but the Lord made me one anyway. He knew and cared about the need of one of His hurting children.

Meeting the Good Shepherd

I am the good shepherd; and I know My sheep. . . . My sheep hear My voice, and I know them, and they follow Me (John 10:14,27 NKJV).

"How can I know that the voice I'm hearing is the voice of God?" someone asks. "What if it's my own inner voice or the voice of the evil one?"

The voice of God is always gentle and full of compassion. And most importantly, it is always consistent with His written Word.

A person of my acquaintance took something that did not belong to her. "I knew it was right because I heard God tell me to do it," she said. If she had tested that voice by the written Word, she would have known she was being deceived by the enemy. God *never* violates His Word. He never contradicts Himself.

Another friend came to me in confusion. "I'm torn between two decisions," she said. "I need to make a choice soon, but I'm not sure which way to go." I suggested one of my favorite Scripture passages—"Let the peace . . . from Christ rule (act as umpire continually) in your hearts . . . settling with finality all questions that arise in your minds" (Colossians 3:15 AMP).

The next day my friend called to say she had made her decision and had wonderful peace regarding it. By letting the peace of Christ "act as umpire" in her heart, she drove out all confusion. God is a God of peace. He desires to make His wishes known to us. He often does this through His Word.

Several years ago I heard a speaker give a teaching on hearing the voice of God. She asked, "How many of you hear the voice of God consistently?" Out of the crowd of hundreds, only a few hands went up. She lead us in a brief relaxation exercise and then said, "Now close your eyes and ask the Lord a question, and listen for His answer."

I asked, "Lord, why do I not hear you more clearly?" Distinctly I heard within, "It's your feeling of self-doubt." I knew He was right. Many of us have been programmed to self-doubt. We are all threatened by a sense of unworthiness.

The Lord is teaching me that through Christ I *am* worthy. God wants us to know the truth about ourselves. Dr. Charles Stanley says, "God wants us to realize our importance in the scheme of His eternal plans and that our peculiarities sometimes hinder us. . . . God wants us to know our position and our supernatural privileges of who we are in Christ."

Every Christian can have an encounter with God. Hearing His voice through His Word or through His Spirit is not for a select few, but for all. As Jesus said, His sheep hear His voice.

Beyond the Impossible

[God] has blessed us in the heavenly realms with every spiritual blessing in Christ. For he chose us in him before the creation of the world. . . . In love he predestined us to be adopted as his sons through Jesus Christ, in accordance with his pleasure and will (Ephesians 1:3-5).

*G*od created you and me to live in His overflowing love. Even before He created the world, He decided to make us His beloved adopted children. Paul understood that. In each of his thirteen letters he said, "Grace and peace to you from God the Father" or something similar.

Peter began his two epistles by saying, "Grace and peace be yours in abundance." Abundance. That's God's overflowing love and grace. That is

76

God's desire for us. Peter goes on to say, "His divine power has given us everything we need for life and godliness through our knowledge of him" (2 Peter 1:3).

I notice that Peter says it is through our knowledge of God that we are able to receive His promised blessings. Our knowledge of God enables us to wait in hope for His abundance to reach us. The psalmist says, "The LORD bestows favor and honor; no good thing does he withhold from those whose walk is blameless" (Psalm 84:11).

Being limited in our understanding, we sometimes wonder why the blessings seem to be withheld. God's timetable does not always agree with ours. He wants us to learn to walk in faith and patience. Since God is God, we can rest assured that His Word is true and that He never makes a mistake. God often has to do a spiritual work in us before we are able to receive the blessings we desire.

One of my friends has undergone severe trials—physically and financially. Still, his letters always contain this sentence: "God is doing a perfect work here." My friend recognizes that God has a purpose in allowing all the things he is experiencing. He yields himself to God's purposes and rests in the knowledge that, as a beloved child of the heavenly Father, he will have his needs supplied.

Looking beyond circumstances enables us to live in hope. Abraham is an example of one who looked beyond what seemed impossible. Abraham waited until he was 100 years old before receiving his promised son, Isaac. "Against all hope, Abraham in hope believed and so became the father of many nations" (Romans 4:18). Our loving Father always keeps His promises.

We've been adopted into the family of God. And, as God inspired Paul to write, "May the God of hope fill you with all joy and peace . . . so that you may overflow with hope by the power of the Holy Spirit" (Romans 15:13).

Living Moment
by Moment

*If we confess our sins, he is faithful
and just and will forgive us our sins
and purify us from all unrighteousness*
(1 John 1:9).

A friend sat across the room from me, eyes
downcast. "No matter what I do," she sighed,
"I feel guilty. My rational mind tells me I'm innocent, but my guilt feelings are weighing me down."

My friend is one of many Christians plagued by
unfounded guilt feelings. They have read the above
verse and turned from their sins, but the truth of
God's forgiveness has not moved beyond intellectual understanding to assurance in their hearts.

Guilt feelings are not all bad. "[Guilt] feelings can stimulate us to change our behavior and seek forgiveness from God and others," Dr. Gary R. Collins explains in his book *Christian Counseling*. "But guilt feelings can also be destructive, inhibitory influences which make life miserable." Such is true of false guilt.

False guilt feelings spring from a variety of incidents ranging in graveness from spending money for a new jacket to the death of a loved one. To be healed of guilt, real or imagined, we must first accept the forgiveness which has already been accomplished through Christ. The other part of healing comes through forgiveness of self.

False guilt feelings often begin in childhood. Christian parents, in a sincere effort to bring up their children to be God-fearing individuals, sometimes set rigid standards impossible for the child to meet. Goals too high for a child to reach leave him feeling like a failure. Self-blame and inferiority feelings often result. Guilt feelings cling to the subconscious mind like dust clinging to the rafters in the attic.

As these children become adults, they take on their parents' attitudes and continue the pattern of expecting the impossible. Dr. Collins says, "Guilt feelings are one of the ways in which we both punish ourselves and push ourselves to keep trying to do better."

A person laden with guilt feelings is lacking in self-worth. He constantly zeroes in on his faults and frailties. Regardless of his achievements, he fails to recognize them. Praise only serves to remind him of his worthlessness. He thinks, "If they only knew what I'm like, they wouldn't applaud me." A guilt-ridden person hasn't learned how to live moment by moment in the freedom of knowing that the Lord accepts him just as he is.

God does not expect perfection of His children. When God said, "Be perfect," He didn't mean *perfect* as we interpret the word. The Greek word for "perfect" is mature or complete. Only God can bring us to completion.

The Light of Assurance

Your eye is the lamp of your body. When your eyes are good, your whole body also is full of light. But when they are bad, your body also is full of darkness (Luke 11:34).

Two women waited in the hospital waiting room. At last the doctor entered. As gently as he could, the doctor explained that the women's sister was in grave condition. She probably would not live more than six months.

One of the sisters began railing at an unfair God who made life miserable for innocent people. The other sister remained calm. "This is not the end," she declared. "It may not be as bad as the doctor thinks. But whatever the outcome, I'll trust God. He has always shown His goodness and mercy to us."

Jesus speaks of the eye as the lamp of the body. When our eyes react to light in a normal manner, our whole body receives the benefit. When our eyes are good and we have proper illumination, we can perform many functions. But if our eyes are impaired so that we can't make use of the light, we're somewhat limited in what we can do.

There is a spiritual parallel. When our eyes are good, they are fixed on Jesus and what He can do. When we have weak spiritual eyes, we are limited in what we see. We are "full of darkness" as the first sister was. The attitude of the second sister showed that her spiritual eyes were strong. She could see through the situation to God's love.

When we hinge our attitudes on the truth that God is loving and caring, we look with good eyes at every situation and circumstance. We see His light surrounding our paths. The assurance that God works out everything for our good gives us a positive outlook on life.

Our problem often is that we have a distorted view of God. We haven't seen Him as He really is. When Jesus lived on this earth He showed us what God is like. "The Son is the radiance of God's glory and the exact representation of his being" (Hebrews 1:3). Jesus went about doing good, always showing mercy and compassion. God is no less compassionate.

He never stands over us to see if we're measuring up but to assure us of His forgiveness.

Some time ago, a young Christian man sat in my living room with his lovely wife. He had been exposed to a great deal of legalism and very little grace. With no reason for it, he felt condemned. The young man knew the Word of God, but he had difficulty seeing its liberating truth.

Christian growth is a process. Our eyes may be weak at first. But as we understand God in the light of His goodness, we begin to see with good eyes.

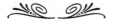

God Never Fails Us

I trust in your unfailing love; my heart rejoices in your salvation (Psalm 13:5).

O my Strength, I sing praise to you; you, O God, are my fortress, my loving God (Psalm 59:17).

I don't understand what's going on in my life," bemoans a friend. "The promises of God seem to be withheld from me. I feel weighted down by cares. God seems far away."

My friend is not alone. "What is wrong?" is a common question. When nothing seems to be lining up the way we think it should, we're prone to question God or to blame ourselves. Often it's nothing we've done or failed to do, and, of course, God is never at fault. Usually our problem is our limited perspective. We see only the immediate circumstances; God sees the whole picture. And He isn't in a hurry like we are.

Along with the positive aspects of the charismatic movement, there are some warped teachings that have been promoted by a few. As a result, some people have been led into believing they can have instant success simply by "claiming" it. God is not calling us to shallow living and quick answers. He is calling for spiritual maturity and disciplined living.

God's aim is to perfect His children. His ways are higher than our ways. He knows what is best for us and when and how to accomplish His purpose in our lives. In bringing us to maturity, He must allow us to experience some situations that we might not choose for ourselves.

David was a man who experienced much trouble. After Samuel anointed him to be king (at about age seventeen), David went back to sheep herding. He didn't ascend the throne until he was thirty years old. During the intervening years, David often had to flee for his life because of the jealous rage of King Saul.

According to many of the psalms which David wrote during those years, he often wondered why God allowed such circumstances to befall him. "How long, O LORD? Will you forget me forever?

How long will you hide your face from me? How long must I wrestle with my thoughts and every day have sorrow in my heart? How long will my enemy triumph over me?" (Psalm 13:1,2).

David dared to express his emotions and to be honest with the Lord about his feelings. In so doing, he was able to rise above his despair. Immediately after expressing his distress, David declared his trust in God: "But I trust in your unfailing love; my heart rejoices in your salvation. I will sing to the LORD, for he has been good to me" (Psalm 13:5,6).

Jo Kimmel says in her book *Steps to Prayer Power* that she now knows "a state of being in which all tragedy, all suffering, all impatience, all anger—before they become these things—are turned into triumphant, creative living." Jo emphasizes that she did not reach that state overnight. From her youth, she disciplined herself to have a meaningful quiet time with the Lord. Jo has experienced times of tragedy, but her awareness of the Lord's presence gave her super-natural strength during those times.

What the Lord did for Jo Kimmel, He will do for you and me. Whatever the extent of our problems, God is greater. For each of us suffering is distinctive, but God will never fail us. We can trust Him in the midst of our trials knowing He will turn them into good if we let Him.

God Is Speaking

My people are destroyed from lack of knowledge (Hosea 4:6).

Reflecting on my years as a schoolteacher, I recall some children who seemed to always listen to everything I said. They were the real students, the learners. They seemed to thirst for knowledge. On the other hand, it seemed that some students hardly ever listened.

I've been thinking how much like those non-listening children we, as God's children, often are. And how much knowledge and how many blessings we miss by our failure to listen to God. It is through Him that we gain our most valuable knowledge and understanding.

Yet, like schoolchildren, our minds are often occupied with the happenings around us. We become

easily distracted by our circumstances and sur-
roundings. We forget that we are the new Israel and
that, through Christ, God's promises are ours. He
asks only that we meet His conditions. By listening
to God and following His instructions, we experience victory.

God is a God of peace. His will for us is peace.
We can have His peace even when life seems to be
in turmoil. But we hear God's voice of peace only
when we listen. Listening requires inner quietness
and discipline. We exercise our wills to listen. We
must set aside time for stillness, time for listening—
regardless of pressures or time's demands.

Webster's definition of "listen" is to hear with
thoughtful attention; to be alert to catch an expected
sound. Listening involves more than our physical
ears. It is hearing with mind and spirit.

When I read my Bible or when I listen to a sermon or Bible teaching, I need to hear with spiritual
ears. I need to be alert and expect the Holy Spirit
to speak to my innermost being. Then I must give
thoughtful attention to what I read or hear.

The more we listen with open minds to the
truths of God's Word, the more meaning is revealed
to us. I read my Bible every day. I often return to
certain verses and meditate on them; I don't want to
miss anything God may be saying to me. God is a

personal God. He sees us as individual persons, and often He has a personal word for us in His written Word. His Holy Spirit speaks to us as we listen with expectancy.

Several years ago I submitted a devotional book manuscript to a certain editor. He promptly returned it, saying, "We don't believe God speaks to people today." Since that man doesn't believe God still speaks, he isn't likely to hear God's voice. Another publisher accepted my book and many are hearing God speak through its pages.

God is speaking to us. Let's not miss His voice.

A Song of Gratitude

*Make a joyful shout to the LORD, all
you lands! Serve the LORD with gladness;
come before His presence with singing.
Know that the LORD, He is God; it is He
who has made us, and not we ourselves;
we are His people and the sheep of His
pasture. Enter into His gates with
thanksgiving, and into His courts with
praise. Be thankful to Him, and bless His
name. For the LORD is good; His mercy is
everlasting, and His truth endures to all
generations* (Psalm 100:1-5 NKJV).

*D*uring my years as a public schoolteacher, reading from the Bible in class hadn't been out-
lawed. Every year near Thanksgiving my pupils

joyfully learned Psalm 100. We often discussed what it meant to give thanks. Today we think of Thanksgiving as a season of the year—but every day should be a day of thanksgiving to God for all His goodness to us.

We take many of our blessings for granted. We who have all five senses have cause for gratitude; some of us have friends who have lost their eyesight or their hearing. We can thank God for our ability to see, hear, taste, smell, and feel.

Sometimes when I listen to the birds sing, I thank God for creating birds to make joyful sounds. I'm thankful for the sounds of music and praise during our church worship services. I'm thankful for the encouraging voices of friends and loved ones.

I'm also thankful for the sense of touch. Some time ago I attended a women's conference where one of the speakers reminded us that we are the body of Christ and that we have the privilege of ministering love to one another through touch. Following her suggestion, we each turned and hugged the person next to us. I had never met the young woman next to me, but I knew she was one of God's children. As we stood in affectionate embrace, tears spilled from her eyes and splashed onto her Bible.

A few hours later, as we were loading our bags into our cars, I met my new friend on the sidewalk.

She flashed a warm smile and said, "Thank you. God bless you." The love in her eyes permeated my being, and a song of gratitude rose in my heart.

Dr. Sidney Simon writes in his book *Caring, Feeling, Touching* that no amount of food can satisfy the human hunger for touch. "It is a hunger for the reaffirming assurance that inside our skins we are 'somebody'; that inside the skins of others, there is 'somebody' just like us."

Everywhere we look, we can find reasons to be thankful. Regardless of what is going on in our lives, we can find something to be thankful for. We may be undergoing unpleasant circumstances, but God's love endures forever.

Following Our Dreams

The kingdom of God does not come with your careful observation, nor will people say, "Here it is," or "There it is," because the kingdom of God is within you
(Luke 17:20,21).

W hat are you looking for?" a man asked his friend when he saw him crawling around on his hands and knees on his lawn late one evening.

"My keys," came the reply.

"Let me help you," his friend offered. "Where did you lose them?"

"In the house."

"In the house! Then why are you looking for them outside?"

"Because it's lighter out here."

That ridiculous story may not be as farfetched as it sounds. Many people are looking outside themselves for the key to life and happiness. Fulfillment comes not from externals but from what is inside us. The kingdom of God and the joy it brings is to be found within.

Do you know the story of the Italian sculptor who saw a block of marble which had been cast aside as worthless? He picked up his hammer and began to chisel away. To those who watched in wonder he said, "I'm unloosing the angel within the marble."

It might be said that we each have an "angel" within us waiting to be loosed. All of us have greater potential than we realize. One of my favorite speakers says, "Each of us is the unique expression of God's creative genius." We haven't taken time to let God show us our supreme value.

It's easier to look outside than to look within. Many of us are educated beyond secondary school, but we still lack the necessary understanding to live joyously. According to experts, 80 percent of our population is unhappy. Why? They do not have a clear picture of who they are and their purpose in life. They're looking outside themselves for the key.

When we have a fever, we don't simply take an aspirin. We try to discover the cause and treat the underlying problem. Unfortunately, we don't always exercise that much wisdom in our spiritual lives. Too often we deal only with symptoms. When disagreeable situations linger, we downgrade ourselves and ask, "Why don't I have more faith?" or "Why can't I be like so-and-so?" without expecting an answer. And we fall into a downward spiral.

We allow our busy lives to shove us onto a merry-go-round where we take little time for solitude and reflection on who we are and how God sees us.

From the time we entered grade school, we have been taught to conform instead of following our dreams. Granted, a degree of conformity is necessary—but God made us unique. He likes variety in our lives just as He does in the flowers He creates.

Much of our unhappiness and many of our problems arise from our failure to understand and accept our own individual personalities. We make the mistake of trying to fit into someone else's mold for us. Until we understand ourselves, we often fail to accept ourselves for the persons we are. God accepts us. He made us with different personalities, dispositions, and abilities.

In his little book *Born Only Once*, Dr. Conrad Baars told the story of a shy little boy who hid under the table, but not entirely out of sight, when the pastor came to visit. No one scolded Johnny or said, "Don't be shy. Be a big boy." They paid no attention to him. When the visitor left, and Johnny came out from under the table, his mother lovingly asked, "Were you shy, Johnny?"

Recalling the incident in adulthood, John said, "That experience gave me a sense of self-confidence and a feeling that I was okay. I'm sure my mother's understanding cured me of much shyness."

Many of us have not been as fortunate as Johnny. We haven't been allowed to grow at our own pace and become what we're supposed to be. Some of us have put "oughts" and "shoulds" on ourselves, expecting things of ourselves that God doesn't expect.

Each of us came into the world with certain innate temperaments. For instance, you are either an introvert or an extrovert. If you are extroverted, you thrive on being with people. You are energized by being with crowds. You may be the "life of the party" on your job or wherever you go. But if you're introverted, you are more successful and energetic when you have limited contact with people.

Another category of opposites is "thinkers" and "feelers." Thinkers are people who prefer to make decisions on the basis of logic, analysis, and objectivity. Feelers are people who prefer subjectivity and personal impact. Feelers let their emotions show. Thinkers, while intellectualizing, may experience intense emotion without showing it. Thinkers and feelers need each other. One is not better than the other. This is the way God made us. When we understand and accept each other, we help each other become better balanced personalities.

As an introverted feeler, I find fulfillment in reading and writing, but I try not to force an extrovert into my mold.

Authors David Kiersey and Marilyn Bates write, "In understanding me you might come to prize my differences from you, and, far from seeking to change me, preserve and even nurture those differences."

When we recognize that the kingdom is within, we'll accept ourselves and each other more fully.

A Day for the Lord

This is the day the LORD has made; let us rejoice and be glad in it (Psalm 118:24).

"W rite Your Own Personal Forecast and Ensure a Good Day." How nice that sounds. But how do we do it? Here are some of my ideas.

To ensure a good day, we need to begin the day on a positive note, knowing that God is with us. Since we live in a world where the very air seems to be permeated with negative thoughts, it isn't always easy to rise above negativity. But we can discipline our minds, tuning out negative thoughts and replacing them with favorable thoughts.

To rejoice during the day, we can choose what we read and listen to. Personally, I begin almost every morning by listening to praise music. That helps me keep my priorities in order. Soon after listening to music, I have a time of Bible reading and prayer.

Throughout the day there are many obstacles that draw our attention away from focusing on the Lord. For some people, television is a snare. A friend had planned an evening filled with tasks that needed immediate attention. When one of her children turned on the television, my friend watched a few minutes to be sure she approved of the program. But an hour later she realized she'd allowed herself to get trapped—she had watched the whole program. Then she found herself frustrated when trying to accomplish all her tasks before bedtime.

Sometimes it's hard for busy people to say no to the daily demands and requests that keep them from fulfilling their goals. We want to help, but we may need to discipline our emotional responses to make them line up for our good. Then there are the times when everything seems to be going against us, and we are tempted to give up. If we give up, we're giving in to our emotional responses and letting them work against us. Emotions in themselves are not wrong; God created us with emotions. However, we need to control our emotional *responses* rather than being controlled by them.

I suggested to a friend who was going through a difficult period that she begin her day by repeating certain Scripture passages. She said, "I never can think of any positive ones when I need them." If you have the same problem, I'd like to suggest some of my favorites:

This is the day the LORD has made; let us rejoice and be glad in it (Psalm 118:24).

The LORD is my shepherd, I shall not be in want (Psalm 23:1).

I can do everything through him who gives me strength (Philippians 4:13).

And we know that in all things God works for the good of those who love him, who have been called according to his purpose (Romans 8:28).

In all these things we are more than conquerors through him who loved us (Romans 8:37).

The LORD is my light and my salvation—whom shall I fear? The LORD is the stronghold of my life—of whom shall I be afraid? (Psalm 27:1).

If we are walking with God, His promises are ours. He desires that we have a good day every day. All He asks is our cooperation. He gives us the privilege of writing our own forecast!

When We
Need Him Most

For as high as the heavens are above the earth, so great is his love for those who fear him (Psalm 103:11).

I stood at my living room window watching two little figures until they disappeared down the street. They looked so small and defenseless against the big world. One was a six-year-old boy, the other a girl almost eight. Each carried a book satchel in one hand and a lunch box in the other.

That scene and similar ones repeated themselves many times through the days, weeks, and years as I reluctantly sent my son and daughter out to face the cold world. Several decades have passed since that first disquieting day when I was required to trust my priceless human treasures to someone else's care for the better part of the day. But I still remember it vividly.

One recent morning, when I was meditating on God's personal love and care for His children, I recalled that day. If I was so desirous (yet incapable) of protecting my children from harm, how much more does God's love and protection extend to us? "Can a mother forget the baby at her breast and have no compassion on the child she has borne? Though she may forget, I will not forget you!" (Isaiah 49:15).

Like every mother, there were many times when I had to be temporarily separated from my children—times when my eyes could not follow them. But you and I are never out of our heavenly Father's sight. The Scriptures tell us again and again that the eyes of the Lord are always on His children.

Being human, my love for my children was conditional. Too often my warmth and affection were based on what my children did or failed to do. Not so with God. His love never depends on our conduct or even upon our attitudes. God's love is determined only by His nature—and His nature is unconditional love.

The psalmist probably understood God's love as well as anyone ever has. He prayed, "Keep me as the apple of your eye" (Psalm 17:8). The apple of the eye is the pupil. How valuable to us is the pupil of our eye. God places even more value on us.

Brennan Manning tells the story of an insecure little boy who grew up in a large family. One day the boy started into the house to get his baseball glove, but he paused outside the door when he heard his father and a neighbor talking. The boy's ears pricked up when he heard the neighbor ask his father, "Of all your thirteen children, do you have a favorite?"

One by one, the father named each child, beginning with the one most lacking in desirable qualities. A daughter was ostracized by her friends because of a physical handicap; a son wanting to be an athlete, was a failure in sports; the oldest son had a problem that led to disgraceful living.

As the father went down the list, describing the shortcoming or deficiency of each child, he added something like, "My heart really goes out to that poor kid." The little boy, eavesdropping at the door, decided, "My father loves the one most who needs him most." Isn't that a facsimile of our heavenly Father's love? When we need Him most, He is present with His love.

When we're tempted to doubt the Lord's presence, we can recall the words of an old hymn by William C. Pool, "Just When I Need Him Most":

Just when I need Him most, Jesus is near,
Just when I falter, just when I fear;
Ready to help me, ready to cheer,
Just when I need Him most.

Just when I need Him, Jesus is strong,
Bearing my burdens all the day long;
For all my sorrow giving a song,
Just when I need Him most.

"Trust Me!"

Casting the whole of your care [all your anxieties, all your worries, all your concerns, once and for all] on Him, for He cares for you affectionately and cares about you watchfully (1 Peter 5:7 AMP).

*H*ow can you be so happy when bad things are happening to you?" one friend asked another. "Anyone else would be grumbling, but you're always smiling."

"Why should I give myself stomach ulcers over something I have no control over?" came the reply. "I have a choice of complaining or trusting God."

When I overheard that conversation, I thought of Moses and the children of Israel. Soon after the Israelites were led out of Egypt, they began complaining to Moses and Aaron. Moses told them,

"You are not grumbling against us, but against the LORD" (Exodus 16:8).

When we grumble about anything, we're manifesting a lack of trust in God. "But how can I keep from grumbling?" a friend asks. "Look what's going on in my life!"

That's a natural reaction for one who does not know the Lord, but it need not be the reaction of you and me. The Lord invites us to cast all our burdens on Him. He's saying to us, "Stop worrying! Trust me. You are in my care."

How grieved we parents would be if our little children worried about how they would be cared for. Their concerns are our concerns. How much more does our heavenly Father concern Himself with whatever is of concern to us?

Learning to cast all our care upon the Lord is a continual process. We grow in our ability to recognize the hand of God in all our affairs—even in our everyday mundane experiences.

Christian growth is a never-ending process—a slow process partly because we are reluctant to practice the teachings of Jesus. Omar Bradley said, "We have grasped the mystery of the atom and rejected the Sermon on the Mount." A significant portion of the Sermon on the Mount is a message of encouragement to trust instead of worry.

More than fifty years ago a minister by the name of Reinhold Niebuhr composed a prayer which later was adopted as the motto of Alcoholics Anonymous. Perhaps we would do well to make it our daily prayer: "O God, give us serenity to accept what cannot be changed, courage to change what should be changed, and the wisdom to distinguish the one from the other."

When we see ourselves—our situations, our past, our present, and our future—as God sees us, we will lose our tendency to worry and complain, and begin casting our cares on Him.

He Delights to Hear Us

So I say to you: Ask and it will be given to you; seek and you will find; knock and the door will be opened to you (Luke 11:9).

I got so frustrated that I felt like quitting. I was writing an article using my newly acquired computer. My words kept skipping off the screen. Would I ever learn how to use this machine? Hadn't I pressed every possible key and tried everything? And nothing had worked. What else was there to try?

At last I remembered I hadn't tried prayer. I closed my eyes and asked the Lord for help. Then I pressed a few keys which I thought I'd already pressed and, without any explainable reason, my problem was solved. Of course the Lord had been there all the time. I'd been so busy I had ignored His presence. When we feel rushed and over-burdened is the very time we need most to remember the Lord's presence.

"I am with you always," is a verse I memorized and quoted often as a preschooler. At the time I was too young to have much concept of the depth of meaning in those words. Decades later, I'm still learning the depth of their reality.

The Lord has promised never to leave us. Yet, we often act as if He has left us. When we're facing a difficult situation, we often forget His promise. Like the disciples of Jesus' day, we tend to forget His power. The same Jesus who stilled the wind and waves on the sea when His disciples were so afraid is present to still the storms in our lives. He concerns Himself not only with big events but even with our little frustrations. He only waits for us to ask.

Too often I get so busy or frustrated that I almost give up on something before remembering to ask the Lord for help. I sometimes rely on my own strength and understanding when the heavenly Father is right there beside me, waiting for me to call on Him. I don't need to wait until frustration hits me before recognizing His presence.

I've found that praying spontaneously through-out the day is just as valuable as my early-morning time when I give myself totally to the Lord in prayer and meditation. All our experiences are important to God. He delights to hear His children pray anytime, and He delights to answer all our legitimate requests.

Cradled in His Arms

*The LORD is my light and my salvation—
whom shall I fear? The LORD is the stronghold of my life—of whom shall I be afraid?*
(Psalm 27:1).

A hunter stood watching a number of hounds chasing a herd of deer in a nearby field. Soon he noticed a young fawn that looked as if it had run as far as it could. Panting and apparently almost out of breath, it seemed to muster extra strength as it neared the fence where the hunter stood. It leaped over the fence rails and crouched at the hunter's feet as if appealing for help. The dogs followed in hot pursuit. The hunter reached down and picked up the little fawn and chased off the dogs.

When I read that story, I thought of you and me and our relationship with God. When we feel desperate and in need of help in a special way, it's as if God picks us up and cradles us in His protective arms. He cares much more for us than a mere man cares for a helpless deer.

Times come in our lives when we wonder how we can manage. "Why did this happen to me?" I remember when many troublous questions bombarded my mind past midnight, when I finally got to bed, after the doctor had set my fractured right wrist. Living alone, I couldn't imagine how I could get along for six weeks with my arm in a cast. My emotional ache was greater than my physical pain.

God, of course, had plans I didn't know about. Thoughtful friends came almost every day for six weeks, bringing food and doing things I couldn't do for myself.

God doesn't prevent trials from coming to His children. But He is present with us and faithful to provide for us. We see examples of His love and care in parents' concern for their children.

"My daughter is crying," whispered the friend standing beside me at a retreat worship service. Carefully stepping over several pairs of feet and across the aisle, she maneuvered her way to her daughter and put her arms around her. I hadn't noticed the young woman's tears, but her mother had.

Others may be unaware of how we're hurting, but our heavenly Father knows. He sees and cares as no earthly parent can. In a spiritual sense, He hastens to our side. He is an "ever-present help in trouble" (Psalm 46:1). As my friend's love was manifested to her daughter, God's love is manifested to us in far greater measure.

Whatever happens to us, God is near. "The LORD Almighty is with us; the God of Jacob is our fortress" (Psalm 46:7). When we have gone as far as our strength will allow, we can remember the Lord's presence. He is our strength.

A Contagious Faith

Wait on the LORD; be of good courage, and He shall strengthen your heart; wait, I say, on the LORD! (Psalm 27:14 NKJV).

I heard on a television program the reason a flock of geese honks as it flies overhead in V-shaped formation. Researchers have found that the geese aren't simply making a noise, as I'd always supposed. They are honking to encourage their leader, the one at the apex of the triangle. It's as if they're saying, "You're doing great. We appreciate you. Keep up the good work."

What a fine example for us humans. There's no one among us who does not benefit from sincere words of encouragement.

In spite of numerous hardships, Paul was an encourager. Paul and some other prisoners were en route to Rome where Paul was to appear before Caesar for preaching the gospel. Before many days passed, it became apparent that the crew was in danger because of a violent storm.

As the days went by, sailing became so hazardous that they threw the cargo and the ship's tackle overboard. Paul says, "When neither sun nor stars appeared for many days and the storm continued raging, we finally gave up all hope of being saved" (Acts 27:20).

Paul could have been angry. He had warned the officers in charge that sailing would be dangerous, but his advice had been disregarded. Now that their situation looked hopeless, Paul encouraged the others with these words, "But now I urge you to keep up your courage, because not one of you will be lost; only the ship will be destroyed" (Acts 27:22).

Moreover, Paul dared to tell the crew that an angel had appeared to him in the night and said, "'God has graciously given you the lives of all who sail with you.' So keep up your courage, men, for I have faith in God that it will happen just as he told me" (Acts 27:24,25).

After two weeks of being too fearful to observe meals, everyone on the ship drew courage from Paul's faith and heeded his appeal to eat. However, a little later, when shipwreck looked imminent, the soldiers wanted to kill the prisoners lest they escape. But the commanding officer, stirred by Paul's position, stopped their plan. In the end everyone on the ship reached land safely.

Paul waited on the Lord, remained confident in Him, and received courage and strength of heart. His faith and courage were so contagious that everyone on board was encouraged. Paul's courage became an answer to their needs.

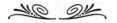

A Restful Journey

Let be and be still, and know (recognize and understand) that I am God (Psalm 46:10 AMP).

*M*ost of us look forward to an occasional trip, perhaps a journey to a scenic, restful spot. We sometimes need to get away from everyday living in order to gain a fresh perspective.

But "the one journey that ultimately matters," says Reverend Gordon Cosby, "is the journey into the place of stillness deep within oneself. . . . At the place of 'central silence,' one's own life and spirit are united with the life and spirit of God."

Many of us, after returning home from a vacation, say that the best part is getting back home. Gordon Cosby says to reach a place of inner stillness is to be at home, and that "to fail to reach it is to be forever restless."

All of us need a time every day when we can enter a place of quiet rest—a time set aside just for ourselves alone, a time to get in touch with our feelings and with God.

A friend asked, "How can we be still and know that God is God?" I have to admit it isn't easy. To know God as He wants us to know Him requires discipline. To know God is to spend time with Him, shutting out all inner and outer distractions.

Our hurry-hurry world says we don't have time to be still. There's too much to be accomplished to sit around listening for the voice of God. But we defeat ourselves if we listen to the voice of the world instead of the voice of God.

One reason we're reluctant to be still is that stillness may force us to face things within that we'd rather not face. Going to a place where no noises prevail, we may be surprised to hear the profuse noise inside our own minds. There have been times when I've had a glimpse of this inner noise when I've gone to bed at night. Everything around me had become still and quiet, but the noise within kept me awake longer than I wanted.

In his book *Digging Deep,* Pastor Robert Schwenk tells about a nervous woman who came to him because her doctor refused to give her any more tranquilizers. She had dumped all her unwanted emotions into her subconscious mind, hoping to keep them locked up. But her feelings were "beginning to raise the lid, and it was taking every ounce of energy she had to keep it all locked up."

When her pastor tried to help her face reality, the woman asked, "Why can't I just be the person I used to be?" She didn't want to face her hidden self, give up resentments, and undergo emotional healing. It is impossible for us to continue being the persons we used to be. We're growing up. As we slow down and get still before the Lord, He will help us if we allow Him to.

It was when Moses slowed down from his disquieting pace of life that God spoke to him at the burning bush in the desert. The late Jamie Buckingham wrote, "We often miss the blessings from burning bushes—the things through which God speaks."

Sometimes it's when we've reached the end of our resources that we are most ready to listen for the voice of God. But we can spare ourselves much inner turmoil if we take time to listen to God before we come to the end of ourselves.

If we had to choose between a literal journey and an inner journey, we'd profit most from the inner journey.

Being True to God

Just as you received Christ Jesus the Lord, so go on living in him—in simple faith. Grow out of him as a plant grows out of the soil it is planted in . . . (Colossians 2:6,7 PHILLIPS).

*P*erfect submission, all is at rest . . ." Sarah sat in the pew, singing with the congregation. But suddenly she stopped and pondered what she was singing. "Forgive me, Lord," she silently prayed. "I've been singing a lie. I'm not at all at rest. My mind is churning like a turbulent stream after a rainstorm. But why, Lord? Why is it that most of the time my mind hops restlessly from one thought to another?"

The peaceful atmosphere of the worship service enabled Sarah to get still enough to hear the answer.

It came so clearly that it startled her. "You're so busy doing things for me and for others that you don't take time to be still and let me love you. You stay too busy to hear me speak."

While the song service continued, Sarah let her mind drift to the words of John 4:24: "God is spirit, and his worshipers must worship in spirit and in truth." Then she recalled another Scripture passage and turned the pages of her Bible until she found it:

> With eyes wide open to the mercies of God, I beg you, my brothers, as an act of intelligent worship, to give him your bodies, as a living sacrifice, consecrated to him and acceptable by him. Don't let the world around you squeeze you into its own mold, but let God remold your minds from within . . . (Romans 12:1,2 PHILLIPS).

"That's it," Sarah said to herself. "I've allowed the world around me to squeeze me into its mold instead of letting God remold my mind from within. The true worship Jesus spoke of in John's gospel doesn't mean constantly *doing* things but being led by His Spirit."

When the service was over, Sarah drove away with renewed vision. She had laid aside the grave clothes of the law and was now robed with a new understanding of Christ's righteousness. She determined to get up a little earlier every morning and take time to hear God's still small voice before beginning her day's activities.

Until that day, Sarah, like many of us, had focused on externals and allowed circumstances to control her life. That's the world's way. The only way to be true to ourselves and to God is to live, not from the outside, but from the inside, handing all our concerns over to God.

To keep myself reminded of that truth, I often read a card I keep in my desk drawer:

When the care or charge of anything
Rests upon you, God ceases to be a God of peace.
Bear not a single care thyself.
One is too much for thee.
The work is mine, and mine alone,
And thine is—
Trust in me.

A Smile from Deep Within

My son, pay attention to what I say; listen closely to my words. Do not let them out of your sight, keep them within your heart (Proverbs 4:20,21).

*T*he secret of happy living is to give yourself all the good news you can, as often as you can." So began the devotional I read one morning. A few days later, in another book, I read similar words: "Tell yourself all the good news you know."

Both authors were referring to setting the tone, not only for a day, but also for life. The words we dwell on become a part of our lives. By our thoughts, we actually attract to ourselves many of the things that happen to us. Nothing keeps our souls and bodies in a healthier state than paying attention to good news and letting our hearts dwell on it.

Just as our physical life has its fountain in the physical heart, so our spiritual life takes its direction from our spiritual heart. Many medical doctors know the truth that Solomon spoke in the Scripture above. John A. Schindler, M.D., wrote, "Healthful living is more a matter of having the right kind of emotions than anything else. . . . The most important aspect of living consists in training and handling our emotions."

Having that knowledge from Scripture and from the medical profession, we are challenged to tell ourselves frequently all the good news we know and to respond to it with joy. Sometimes we may feel that we have no good news to tell ourselves. That's a good time to recall the words of the old hymn "Count Your Blessings" by Johnson Oatman, Jr.:

> When upon life's billows you are tempest-tossed,
> When you are discouraged, thinking all is lost,
> Count your many blessings, name them one
>   by one,
> And it will surprise you what the Lord
>   hath done.

A few years ago I had the privilege of attending a retreat in North Carolina. People of all ages and

125

denominations gathered on a wooded college campus for a time of spiritual refreshing. Five or six of the most joyous people there were in wheelchairs. They know that unless the Lord works a miracle in their bodies they'll be confined to a wheelchair the rest of their lives. But I never saw any of them without a smile—a smile that came from deep within.

The most joyful of the group was not only confined to a wheelchair, but was unable to speak. He responded with a smile or a gesture of his head or hand to everything said to him. I was told that the young man has a brilliant mind and holds a good job. He is not allowing his peculiar disease to sap his joy or keep him from making goals and plans for the future.

Some individuals have a layer of fundamental emotions that naturally are cheerful. But not everyone does. Many of us have to work at keeping our minds in tune by frequently telling ourselves good news.

I've read that the American philosopher Henry David Thoreau used to lie in bed for several minutes every morning, telling himself all the good news he could think of. Most of us spend a considerable amount of time every morning preparing our bodies for the day, but forget that preparing our souls is just as important.

Dr. Schindler said we need to carry one positive thought and hang it like a big sign over the state of our minds. I find the best way for me to do that is to find a Bible promise that applies to me and meditate on it throughout my day.

In his book *Centering on the Lord Jesus*, George Maloney writes, "You need to take deliberate steps daily to remember the presence of [Jesus] and to experience the constant love that Jesus brings to you as He intimately dwells within you through His Holy Spirit."

We might do well to pray for ourselves as Paul did for the Thessalonians: "May the Lord direct your hearts into God's love . . . " (2 Thessalonians 3:5).

Precious Sorrows

He was despised and rejected by men, a man of sorrows, and familiar with suffering (Isaiah 53:3).

Although he was a son, he learned obedience from what he suffered (Hebrews 5:8).

I received a book entitled *Don't Waste Your Sorrows* by Paul E. Billheimer. When I read the subtitle, *A study in sainthood and suffering*, I promptly placed the book on the shelf. "Who wants to arrive at sainthood via suffering?" I asked myself. "Not I!" So the book remained on my shelf for some time.

I've learned that we're not often given a choice in the matter of suffering. The writer of the foreword of Dr. Billheimer's book says pain and suffering are not an oversight or accident, but "part of the eternal love plan of God for perfecting 'His family' on earth for their place in the eternal Kingdom of God." God's purpose is to bring His children to spiritual maturity.

Nowhere does the Bible teach that God is the author of pain and suffering. But when sorrow comes, God is able to sustain us in it and use it for our blessing. There is no escape on this earth from a certain amount of suffering, but we do have a choice of how we handle it.

During the time of my life when I suffered most, I found great comfort in knowing that Jesus suffered and that He understood and cared about my pain. I was also helped by recalling the words of a song:

> It is not mine to question
> the judgments of my Lord,
> It is but mine to follow
> the leadings of His Word.

How prone we are to question God. But the correct question is not, "Why, Lord?" but "Lord, what do You want to teach me from this situation?" To ask *why* is to waste our sorrows. To yield to the hand of the Lord is to allow Him to redeem the hurt and bring forth good from it.

The psalmist, who went through tremendous emotional suffering, said, "It was good for me to be afflicted so that I might learn your decrees" (Psalm

119:71). Affliction teaches us lessons we can learn in no other way. I join Dr. Billheimer in saying, "I have learned more about God in my time of sore testing than at any other period of my life."

Dr. Charles L. Allen says sorrows are precious possessions. He explains that God "does not deliberately create calamity, send disease, cause wrecks and all the other things that hurt and destroy." God does permit certain things to happen. We can choose to allow those things to make us bitter and resentful or to make us better Christians.

Remember the true story of H.G. Spafford? After making arrangements to take his family by ship to Europe, Mr. Spafford was detained in Chicago. He sent his wife and four little girls on. The ship crashed into another vessel in the Atlantic and split in two. Mrs. Spafford was rescued, but the little girls were lost at sea.

When the sad news reached Mr. Spafford, he joined his wife as soon as possible. Soon thereafter he wrote a song many of us have sung in our churches:

It Is Well with My Soul

When peace, like a river, attendeth my way,
When sorrows like sea billows roll;

Whatever my lot, Thou hast taught me to say,
It is well, it is well with my soul.

Though Satan should buffet, tho' trials
   should come,
Let this blest assurance control,
That Christ has regarded my helpless estate,
And hath shed his own blood for my soul.
It is well with my soul,
It is well, it is well with my soul.

In an almost unbelievable way, this hurting
father was able to turn tragedy into triumph.

Suffering can clarify our vision of God. It can
open our eyes to see more clearly God's loving nature. Suffering is never without purpose. How we
are affected by it depends on how we accept it.

The Secret of Joy

I will see you again and you will rejoice,
and no one will take away your joy
(John 16:22).

*I*f the Christian life is supposed to be one of joy,
why don't we more consistently manifest greater
joy? Is it, as the TV commercials would lead us to believe, that we need to acquire more *things?* No. The
English poet William Cowper expressed it in these
words:

> Happiness depends, as Nature shows,
> Less on exterior things than most suppose.

Is it that we're living in the wrong place? No,
again. Another English poet, Edward Young, wrote:

> True happiness is to no place confined,
> But still is found with a contented mind.

Is joy lacking because we fail to seek it? Popular writer Henry Van Dyke believed the opposite: "We cannot find happiness until we forget to seek for it."

Could it be that we are to find joy in the midst of pain? Are there some lessons we must learn on the road to happiness? Edward Young answers *yes* to both questions:

> Every life has its joy; every joy its law.
> May heav'n ne'er trust my friend with
>   happiness
> Till it has taught him how to bear it well
> By previous pain; and made it safe to smile!

My mother was 83 when she went to her eternal home. Because of failing health, she had to spend the last few years of her life in a nursing home. The last time I saw her before her departure from earth, Mother was radiant. She clapped her hands and said, "I know it's ridiculous but I feel such joy!"

Ridiculous in the eyes of the world, but not to us who knew her. Mother had learned to find her joy in

133

the Lord. She could join the psalmist in saying, "Your comforts delight my soul" (Psalm 94:19 NKJV).

An elderly woman in our church was confined to her bed the last several years of her life. She was an inspiration to all who her knew her. We who went to encourage her came away ourselves encouraged. With joy, she often said, "I want to live as long as the Lord allows, so I can continue to pray for others."

Did that woman and my mother know a secret that you and I need to know? What they knew was never meant to be hidden. They simply knew and lived by Jesus' words, "I have told you this so that my joy may be in you and that your joy may be complete" (John 15:11).

What Jesus had told the disciples was that He was the vine and they were the branches. As branches are united to the vine, so our joy is linked to our understanding of our union with Christ.

Apart from this teaching of Jesus, abiding joy is lacking. Moments of happiness may come, but until we realize that we are in union with Christ, our joy is likely to be short-lived. As the branches receive their life from the vine, we receive an uninterrupted flow of life from Christ, our vine. And in His life is joy.

The joy of Jesus is divine. Until we find the joy of the Lord, we may look for artificial joy. We may seek pleasure in material things and be bound by the limitations of the world. Life in Christ is meant to awaken in us a new kind of joy—divine joy not dependent on circumstances. This heavenly joy is a free gift from God.

Desires of
the Heart

"I know the plans I have for you," declares the LORD, "plans to prosper you and not to harm you, plans to give you hope and a future" (Jeremiah 29:11).

A prominent minister said if we are living in faith, we will prepare to live to be one hundred years old. Then he asked two questions: "What goals do you have today? What good do you wish to accomplish?" Regardless of whether we plan to live to the age of one hundred, we are to live today—and every day—knowing God has a plan and a purpose for us.

In order to have a satisfying life, we need goals. Every day can count for God. However, it is healthy to realize that God usually is not in as great a hurry as we are. As minister and author Jamie Buckingham reminded us, "It is never God's will for a man of God to burn himself out, even in service for God. God does not want us to overtax our machinery. . . . He causes clouds to pause, commands a Sabbath rest, and smiles when His servants slow down and relax."

Resting in God, we find His will within us. His will is often revealed in the secret desires of our hearts, the very things we find the most satisfaction in doing. Our talents were given to us by God to fulfill His purpose through us.

That doesn't mean we won't experience disappointments, frustrations, and delays along the way. Ten or twelve years ago, I was disappointed when an editor kept my book manuscript for eight months, then returned it, saying his company had decided not to publish it. Several months later I realized God was in that situation for my good. I read that the particular publishing company was in financial difficulty. Before too long, I found another publisher, and I've been pleased with the results.

Sometimes we attempt to do something, and when it fails we blame circumstances. But God often has a hand in it. When Paul and his companions planned to go to Asia to preach, something arose to prevent their going. Then they tried to go to

Bithynia, and again they were stopped. Luke wrote that on both occasions the Holy *Spirit* kept them from going (Acts 16:6,7). We're not told why, but we know it was for a good reason.

When we face trials and disappointments, we would do well to recognize God's hand in the situation and remember He has not forgotten the plans He has for us. He will see that those plans are fulfilled if we rely on Him.

Hidden
Possibilities

*Looking away [from all that will dis-
tract] to Jesus, Who is the Leader and
the Source of our faith. . . . Just think of
Him . . .* (Hebrews 12:2,3 AMP).

*V*isitors to the woodcarver's shop shook their
heads in wonderment. Slabs of timber lay
sprawled about the workshop. "How can you make
anything out of all this?" they asked. "And how do
you decide what to carve out of each piece?"

The woodcarver was confident. "I carefully
selected each piece of timber during my journeys
through neighboring hills," he explained. "When
I'm ready to carve something, I just look at a piece of

wood and it seems to suggest what it should become—a rabbit, a deer, an eagle. . . ."

What made the difference between what the woodcarver saw and what his visitors saw? The woodcarver had *carefully selected* the timber he chose to use. He had trained his eyes to see possibilities in the wood. His visitors looked around and saw nothing but heaps of worthless timber.

There was a time when I looked at my life and saw only a heap of worthlessness. How could God make anything useful out of me? There had been so many distractions from what I had supposed my life should be.

One day, when I felt especially hopeless, I picked up my Amplified Bible and it fell open to the twelfth chapter of Hebrews. Verses two and three leaped out at me. After pondering those verses, I realized I could look away from every distraction, every negative, and all the seeming impossibilities, and just focus on Jesus.

Like the woodcarver, Jesus had carefully selected the "timber" that had gone into my life. He knew why He chose it, and He knew He could make something useful and beautiful out of it.

The Lord "has given us new birth into a living hope," says Peter (1 Peter 1:3). The One who gave us a living hope lives within us. His ministry includes producing hope in our hearts and optimism when outward situations spell negativism.

Theologian Kenneth Wuest wrote, "In view of the fact that the Holy Spirit is producing in the Christian's heart that buoyant spirit of hopefulness, it is the responsibility of that Christian to put out of his mind everything that would disturb Christian optimism which always hopes for the best and looks on the bright side of things."

Oswald Chambers says, "If we are haunted [inhabited] by God, nothing else can get to us, no cares, no tribulations, no anxieties." That doesn't mean that we'll have no cares or tribulations. But if we fix our eyes on the Lord, as the writer to the Hebrews advises, we will see Jesus' hand in our concerns and trust Him to work in them.

Do Not
Be Afraid

*Teach me your way, O L<small>ORD</small>; lead me in a
straight path* (Psalm 27:11).

*T*wo roads converged in a wood, and I—
    I took the one less traveled by,
    And it has made all the difference.

So ends philosophical poet Robert Frost's poem,
"The Road Not Taken."

Many times you and I come to a path or cross-
road in our spiritual walk. Shall we take the path
most traveled or shall we dare to venture out on the
one least traveled? Does an unseen force beckon us
onto the least traveled path? Could that unseen force
be God?

We may hear Him whisper, "Come, I'll be with you." By choosing His path, we may discover, as the poet did, that "it has made all the difference." It can make all the difference in our spiritual growth.

The smooth, well-beaten path where we see many others traveling may look friendlier or more exciting. But most likely, it will not lead to the overcoming life the Lord has planned for us. Jesus said, "For many are invited, but few are chosen" (Matthew 22:14). Could He have been suggesting that He chooses only those who accept the narrow road, the road less traveled?

The road less traveled sometimes looks foreboding. And something within our frail nature causes us to shrink from the narrow road. But the sooner we accept the fact that the circumstances of life are not easy, the less difficult our lives become. That is, we begin to learn to pay less attention to circumstances and focus more on the Lord.

I received a note from a friend who has had a series of trials, her most recent being a physical one. She wrote, "This illness gives me an opportunity to 'Be still and know that God is God.'" My friend is learning that the Christian path may be full of pain as well as joy. It's also a growing time. The greatest tragedy of life is not that we suffer pain and calamity, but that we fail to learn the lessons contained in them.

There have been times in my life when I've cried, "God, get me out of this!" But eventually I was glad He didn't. God's grace is sufficient. To put off dealing with problems that confront us is to postpone the spiritual growth and blessing the Lord has for us. Our all-wise, all-loving Father knows where He is leading us and why. His promises will sustain us in every situation. We can rest assured that His purposes are always good.

Wherever we are on our spiritual path, we can receive this word from God: "Be strong and courageous. Do not be afraid" (Deuteronomy 31:6).

Victorious!

Consider it pure joy, my brothers, whenever you face trials of many kinds
(James 1:2).

*P*lease pray that God will get me out of this situation," a friend wrote. But I didn't feel led to pray that way. Instead, I prayed that the Lord would strengthen her and do whatever was best for her. And He did. My friend now knows God's blessing in her trial.

Many Christians view trials as inconsistent with joy and with the teachings of Jesus that He came to give us abundant life. But all Scripture must be understood in the light of other Scriptures and never isolated.

It is through trials that we grow in faith and Christlikeness. "The life of faith," says Oswald Chambers, "is something infinitely further on than sanctification, of faith tried and proved and has stood the test."

For some time I corresponded with a woman who felt that her world had crumbled. She saw no way out of her despair. As we continued corresponding, her letters were bathed in fewer and fewer tears. Finally I received a letter written on cheery yellow stationery. It began, "Each new day brings a new way to praise the Lord." Her circumstances had not changed, but she had.

God is in the business of putting lives back together. He does not always do it the way we expect Him to, but He always does it in the way that's best for us.

As long as we live in this world, trials will come. The men and women of the Bible did not escape them. Jesus certainly did not. He voluntarily went through suffering so that you and I can be victorious in the midst of our trials.

God can bring good out of anything and everything. Many circumstances befall us that we cannot understand. From these things we can learn valuable spiritual lessons. Positive things come from all that happens to us *if* we release them to God.

A friend wrote that he is learning that when he is in a dark place he can rely on the light God gives him. "When circumstances don't change, my attitude toward them does," he wrote. "I can accept them. God gives me the constant awareness that He is my Rock and my Shield. Regardless of what comes, He is there. He is my life. I can stand on His promises."

Whatever we go through, we can experience the same kind of victory my friend is experiencing. Blessings are in store for us when we keep trusting in the One who is willing and able to help us. Somewhere I read this poem:

> Out of the presses of pain
> Cometh the soul's best wine;
> And the eyes that have shed no rain
> Can shed no shine.

Spiritual Stars Shining Brightly

And now, dear friends of mine, I beg you not to be unduly alarmed at the fiery ordeals which come to test your faith, as though this were some abnormal experience. You should be glad, because it means that you are called to share Christ's sufferings (1 Peter 4:12,13 PHILLIPS).

"Why man suffers isn't a difficult question to deal with if you see it from God's perspective," says Gene Edwards in his book *The Inward Journey*. Our problem is that it takes such a long time to reach the place where we see suffering from God's broad viewpoint instead of from our limited perspectives.

Several years ago, when I was experiencing a personal trial, some of my friends offered the type of sympathy I did not need. One day I quoted to one such friend these words of David: "It was good for me to be afflicted so that I might learn your decrees" (Psalm 119:71). She looked at me in disbelief until I showed her the reference in the Bible.

"It takes the darkness of the night to bring out the beauty of the stars, and it takes the clouds and the storm to bring out the glories of the rainbow," said John R. Church in a radio talk. It's when we're going through soul darkness that we are able to see God's spiritual stars shining brightly upon us.

Until we go through sorrow, we may take the spiritual dimension of life too lightly. We may be prone to feel self-sufficient. God wants to bring us to the point of recognizing our own helplessness and our supreme need of Him.

God's purpose is to bring us to a place of drinking deeply of Him, a place where we recognize His hand in everything. That we see Him, not as a faraway God, but as an indwelling, comforting presence, is the Father's aim for His children.

A good example of one who viewed suffering from God's perspective is Joseph Ton, a former pastor in Rumania. At one time the secret police orchestrated a vicious campaign against him.

Anonymous, scandalous letters were sent to his church members. Reverend Ton recalled these words from Scripture: "You also, like living stones, are being built into a spiritual house . . ." (1 Peter 2:5). Then he said, "I must have some rough corners that need chipping off. These troublemakers are not my enemies. They are my Father's stone cutters."

Reverend Ton could have viewed the unjust attacks as insurmountable problems. Instead, he chose to accept them as opportunities for his spiritual growth toward perfection.

Gene Edwards wrote, "As a believer it is given to you to enter in a small way, into a portion of the cross of Jesus Christ." The cross of Jesus was the price He paid to do the will of the Father so that others could be blessed. Our cross may be to go through the fire of suffering. Others may then receive the blessing of comfort through us.

Oswald Chambers said it is suffering that squeezes the grapes that produce the wine for others. Can you and I accept the painful privilege of being made into wine to quench the thirst of others who are hurting?

Helen Steiner Rice wrote:

> There's a lot of comfort in the thought
> That sorrow, grief, and woe

Spiritual Stars Shining Brightly

Are sent into our lives sometimes
To help our souls to grow. . . .
For through the depths of sorrow
Comes understanding love,
And peace and truth and comfort
Are sent from God above.

The Gift
of Emotion

*"In your anger do not sin": Do not let
the sun go down while you are still angry*
(Ephesians 4:26).

I walked unnoticed into a place of business and
heard the proprietors screaming at each other.
Each was blaming the other for a mistake. I waited,
praying silently for peace to enter their hearts and
permeate the atmosphere. Soon the pair lowered
their voices and began talking reasonably. In a few
minutes they were conversing as if nothing had happened between them.

Many years ago my reaction to such an episode
might have been one of condemnation. But those
two persons probably did just what they needed to

do—got their feelings out into the open instead of bottling them up to seethe and explode later.

When God created us, He endowed us with emotions and the ability to feel. Some of us feel more deeply than others. That is, our emotions respond or react strongly to our inner world and to the world round us.

Dr. Conrad Baars explains in his book, *Healing Your Emotions,* that a person who always appears "cool and collected" may be dangerously suppressing his emotions. A mature person has a harmonious integration between emotions, thoughts, and will. Our emotions need to be recognized and accepted—not regarded as a liability. We need only to learn how to deal with our emotions.

Jesus Himself expressed emotions such as anger and frustration. Remember how he looked around in anger when the Pharisees in the synagogue wanted to indict Him for healing a man's hand on the Sabbath? (Mark 3:5)

Much is said about the emotion of anger. Dr. James Dobson differentiates between acceptable and unacceptable anger. In his book *Emotions: Can You Trust Them?* he suggests that responses produced by extreme fatigue, embarrassment, frustration, and rejection have the earmarks of anger but "have nothing to do with sinful behavior."

Dr. Dobson defines unacceptable anger as "that which motivates us to hurt our fellowman—when we want to slash and cut and inflict pain on another person."

Emotions in themselves are not wrong. They are simply indicators of what we have within. We need not condemn ourselves for fluctuating emotions. When we are angry, we may need to ask the Lord why we feel as we do. He may show us something deep within ourselves which we need to deal with.

We need to learn how to handle our emotions and not allow them to swallow us up. Contrary to the opinion of some, emotions are not automatically taken care of when we accept Christ as Savior. Handling our emotions is often a growth process, just as our walk with the Lord is a matter of growth. Let's never condemn ourselves for our feelings, but allow ourselves to be human.

When we're experiencing emotional pain due to some injurious situation, we need especially to give ourselves permission to be human and to be kind to ourselves. It's all right to release our feelings through tears as long as we don't give in to self-pity. All feelings are valid, and if we are to be emotionally healthy, we need to give them space instead of fighting them or imposing impossible "oughts" and "shoulds" upon ourselves. Emotional energy needs an outlet. Vacuuming the floors or crying on the shoulder of an understanding friend may be helpful.

Whether anger or some other emotion, we can let our emotions make us miserable or we can respond to them positively. Understanding that the Lord is working in our lives gives us a basis for patience with ourselves. By taking ourselves *less* seriously and taking God *more* seriously, we can more effectively handle our unwanted feelings. Whatever our feelings, God understands and is *for* us.

Easing the Pain

We are hard pressed on every side, but
not crushed; perplexed, but not in despair
(2 Corinthians 4:8).

My friend sat across the room from me, her face bathed with tears. "I never dreamed anything like this would happen to me," she sobbed. "I always thought such things happened only to other people."

Into all our lives eventually come tests and trials we'd like to escape. Various pressures, severe illness, disappointments, death, separation, divorce—such crises are the common lot of us all.

Trials can be wonderful learning opportunities. The Chinese word for *crisis* means danger and opportunity. That sounds like a paradox, but it isn't. A crisis is dangerous because it threatens to overwhelm us. It often involves the loss of someone or something we hold dear. At the same time, it is an opportunity because it provides a challenge to rise above circumstances and change and grow.

Crises are turning points that will bring either spiritual maturity or deterioration—depending on how we respond. We can better handle our crises when we remember that others in this day and in Bible times have experienced crises similar to ours. We also need to remember that God does not cause suffering, but He permits it. He has a purpose in it. He will not let it last forever.

How can we handle crises? I have discovered that one of the best ways is to find meaningful promises in the Bible, then underline them and meditate on them. I sometimes concentrate on these promises to the exclusion of other Bible reading until I'm over the pain of the crisis. In the midst of a crisis is no time to run a marathon through the Bible.

Getting over the pain of a crisis may be speeded up by finding something creative to do. We must not withdraw from life and into ourselves. Life goes on in spite of unfortunate happenings. Facing the future is easier when we have a worthwhile project to devote ourselves to.

God has endowed each of us with talents. Daring to toy with various ideas, we may uncover abilities

157

and capacities we never dreamed we possessed. Giving ourselves to such projects can ease the pain of crisis.

Crises are often painful, but if we could not feel pain, neither could we feel joy. Pain, even more than joy, adds meaning and depth to life. For God not only provides the resources to endure pain but uses it to enrich our lives.

In her book *The Spiritual Adventure*, Madame Jean Guyon writes, "Each change in your inward experience or external condition is a new test by which to try your faith and love and will be a help towards perfecting your soul, if you receive it with love and submission."

Waiting Through the Storm

I waited patiently for the LORD; he turned to me and heard my cry. . . . He put a new song in my mouth, a hymn of praise to our God (Psalm 40:1,3).

❧

I had just boarded the plane when the voice of the pilot came over the loudspeaker: "Take your seats quickly and buckle your seat belts. There's a storm approaching, and we want to take off ahead of the storm." So instead of the usual wait, we were soon rolling down the runway and then flying through the air. It was easy. All we had to do was sit back, relax, and trust our pilot.

Spiritually, we are not always able to "take off ahead of the storm." It's not that easy. But we can learn to relax and trust our heavenly Pilot to be with us in the storm and to get us safely through it. God is more in control of the circumstances of our lives than the pilot is in control of the aircraft.

Oswald Chambers said, "Nothing happens in any particular [situation] unless God's will is behind it, therefore you can rest in perfect confidence in Him. Resting in the Lord does not depend on external circumstances at all, but on your relationship to God Himself."

Throughout His walk on earth, Jesus experienced storms—both literal and spiritual. But knowing who He was and His purpose on earth, He relaxed in the storms.

One night Jesus was not with His disciples when they encountered a storm on the lake. About three miles from shore, the disciples saw a figure walking on the water. They were terrified. But the familiar voice of Jesus came across the water, "It is I; don't be afraid." They took Him into the boat and the boat immediately reached shore.

We may be fearful of circumstantial storms, but if we'd listen we might hear Jesus say, "It is I; don't be afraid." Every storm has a purpose—for our good. Sometimes the purpose is to teach us patient reliance on Him. It may be to purify us. Gene Edwards writes, "What you see and feel so painfully may be the Lord's effort to polish a stone."

A friend called me in tears because she had been let down by the person who meant the most to her. After a few minutes, I assured her God would work it out for her good. "I know," she replied, "but what am I to do in the meantime?"

My words probably sounded empty to her, but I could only remind her of the psalmist's words: "I waited patiently for the LORD; he turned to me and heard my cry" (Psalm 40:1). Knowing that, in His own way and in His own time, God will work everything out for our good, we can relax in the storm and wait patiently for Him as the psalmist did.

The Art
of Tranquillity

The LORD is my rock, my fortress and my deliverer; my God is my rock, in whom I take refuge. He is my shield and the horn of my salvation, my stronghold (Psalm 18:2).

*I*f I could only move away from this city of noise, confusion, and stress, I could get over my tensions," a man complained to his minister-friend. "The very air is filled with tension. I'd like to move to the country where I could enjoy quiet meadows and babbling brooks."

"You would find the same tension there," the minister replied. "The tension is not in the air; it's in your mind."

We might disagree with the reply of the minister. Quiet meadows and babbling brooks do sound like a cure for surplus tension. However, we have to admit that a move to a different location is not always the answer. Anyway, most of us don't have the option of moving to the country.

We need to learn how to live peacefully in this age of anxiety. Some stress is normal and necessary to keep us energized. But when we fail to manage our stress, our stress manages us. And life may become miserable.

Stress is not necessarily caused by outside sources. Just as the kingdom of God is within, as Jesus said, so everything else in our lives comes from what we have within. That's why it's so important that we take time to feed daily on the Word of God and upon thoughts that build us up.

The most peaceful and happy people are not necessarily those who live in the most beautiful places, enjoy the best health, or own the most wealth. They have learned how to extract beauty from the mundane. They have learned the art of tranquillity.

On spring mornings, when I was a child, I delighted in looking out our kitchen window to see the lustrous morning glories greeting me from the trellis. But their beauty never lasted. As soon as the warmth of the sun evaporated the dew drops, the delicate blossoms closed for the day.

The world's trappings are like that. The things of the world can never be depended on to supply lasting peace and joy. What we *have* brings only temporary happiness. What we *are* can bring eternal joy.

Lasting happiness revolves on patterns of tranquil thoughts. And our habitual thoughts determine what we become. Solomon wrote "For as he thinks in his heart, so is he" (Proverbs 23:7 NKJV). We cannot think our problems away, but we can learn to recognize the presence of God in our circumstances and receive peace.

God is indeed our rock and our fortress, as the psalmist said.

More Than Conquerors!

In the world you have tribulation and trials and distress and frustration; but be of good cheer [take courage; be confident, certain, undaunted]! For I have overcome the world. [I have deprived it of power to harm you and have conquered it for you] (John 16:33 AMP).

*O*ne of my friends is heavy-hearted because of her sister's ill-fortune. She had to have a leg amputated. It seems so unfair for a devout Christian to have to go through such an ordeal. We cannot understand it. Yet, we know that Jesus told us to expect trials and tribulations.

Troubles can never separate us from God's love. The apostle Paul wrote, "For I am convinced that neither death nor life, neither angels nor demons, neither the present nor the future . . . nor anything else in all creation, will be able to separate us from the love of God that is in Christ Jesus our Lord" (Romans 8:38,39).

God's love empowers us to be more than conquerors. We can be victorious in the midst of trials. It is often in experiencing things we'd rather not experience that we come to know more fully the love of Christ.

It helps to remind ourselves that God's ultimate purpose is to bring us to maturity—to transform us to His image. "If we are truly to cooperate with the transformation of our soul, we must have the courage to face pain and suffering," says Mary C. Coelho in an article in *Weavings* magazine. Looking beyond the problem to what God is accomplishing in our lives enables us to view the situation from God's perspective.

Referring to our trials as *wilderness experiences*, Jamie Buckingham wrote, "The only time a wilderness experience becomes a tragedy is when we fail to understand that the purpose of adversity is to force us to look to God." Our problems will not

remain with us forever. When their purpose
is accomplished, they will pass and we will be
stronger.

We can look beyond our problem and recognize
God's loving hand in it, knowing He may be preparing us to be a blessing to someone else. One day
when I was feeling down, I was blessed by a phone
call from a friend. She gave me this quote from
Oswald Chambers: "If you are going to be used by
God, He will take you through a multitude of experiences that are not meant for you at all. They are
meant to make you useful in His hands, and to
enable you to understand what transpires in other
souls so that you will never be surprised at what you
come across."

The best counselors are not those who have
sailed through tranquil lakes, but those who have
waded through stormy waters. Years ago, when
I was in special need of encouragement, I found
that those who had weathered some storms themselves had much more to offer than those whose
paths had been strewn with roses. God needs
"wounded healers" to help others look beyond their
problem to the problem solver. God can use everything that happens to us as a channel of blessing to
someone else.

Somewhere I came across this little poem written by a man named Gilbert:

> When God is our Companion,
> As we walk the road of life,
> There is help for every problem
> And grace for care and strife!
> And we'll find that we've been happy
> All along the path we've trod,
> When in faith we've made the journey
> Hand-in-hand along with God.

Living Above Defeat

Hope deferred makes the heart sick,
but a longing fulfilled is a tree of life
(Proverbs 13:12).

Against all hope, Abraham in hope
believed . . . (Romans 4:18).

*H*ope springs eternal in the human breast,
Man never is but always to be blessed.

These words were penned by eighteenth-century Alexander Pope. If Mr. Pope were living today, I wonder if he might be tempted to retract the first line of his couplet. So many feelings of hopelessness abound—even among Christians. Many have lost hope, even for future blessings.

Now is a time for hope, perhaps more than any other time in history. If what we hope for is slow in coming, we are to keep on hoping. God is for us; He is working things out for us.

Most of us go through times when God seems far away and all reason for hope seems lost. But God has planted hope and faith in every heart. It's up to us to root out negative thinking and exercise our God-given faith and hope.

When unwanted circumstances loom before us, it is not easy to keep our eyes on the promises of God and keep on hoping. But it's the only way to live above defeat. A first-century Roman writer, Pliny, wrote, "Hope is the pillar that holds up the world." Indeed it is hope in God that sustains and energizes us. Our *faith* in God prompts us to hope in His promises.

Have you ever tried talking to yourself when your hope is low? The psalmist didn't hesitate to talk to himself: "Why are you downcast, O my soul? Why so disturbed within me? Put your hope in God, for I will yet praise him, my Savior and my God" (Psalm 42:5).

In times of desperation, David not only talked to himself but expressed his faith in God: "No one whose hope is in you will ever be put to shame" (Psalm 25:3). A little later we find him again talking to his soul: "Find rest, O my soul, in God alone; my hope comes from him" (Psalm 62:5). Then he declares, "He alone is my rock and my salvation; he is my fortress, I will not be shaken" (Psalm 62:6).

I notice three things about David's affirmations. They are stated in the first person singular—"I" and "my." They are stated in the present tense—"is." They are stated positively.

David repeatedly sets an example for us. He *chose* to be hopeful. Regardless of his circumstances, David praised God. He said, "I will extol the LORD at all times; his praise will always be on my lips" (Psalm 34:1).

When hope is burning dimly in our hearts, let's fan the flame. God can renew our hope and restore our joy.

Peace, Strength, and Encouragement

Fear not, for I have redeemed you; I have summoned you by name; you are mine. When you pass through the waters, I will be with you; and when you pass through the rivers, they will not sweep over you. When you walk through the fire, you will not be burned; the flames will not set you ablaze (Isaiah 43:1,2).

During the last several years I've prayed with many individuals who were passing through fires and floods—spiritual, emotional, and physical. As children of God we are in covenant relationship with the Father. And He declares, "I will not violate my covenant or alter what my lips have uttered"

172

(Psalm 89:34). Regardless of what is happening in our lives, we can be sure God loves us. He says, "I will maintain my love to him forever, and my covenant with him will never fail" (Psalm 89:28).

The early Israelites were as human as you and I. They experienced times of darkness, doubt, and fear. God promised them (as He does you and me), ". . . I will guide them; I will turn the darkness into light before them and make the rough places smooth. These are the things I will do; I will not forsake them" (Isaiah 42:16).

On one occasion, Joshua felt as if he and his people would surely be destroyed by their enemies. He fell on his face and cried out to the Lord. The Lord answered, "Stand up! What are you doing down on your face?" (Joshua 7:10). Then the Lord explained why the Israelites could not stand against their foes. When the matter was taken care of the victory was won.

Remembering the covenant promises of God, and knowing we have access to those promises, fortifies us with peace, strength, and encouragement. When Jacob was fleeing from his angry brother Esau, the Lord appeared to him in a dream and said, "I am with you and will watch over you wherever you go. . . . I will not leave you until I have done what I have promised you" (Genesis 28:15).

173

Sometimes we may wish we could flee from a certain person or situation. The Lord is saying to us, as He said to Jacob, "I am with you and will watch over you." And as He said to Joshua on a critical occasion, He says to us, "Have I not commanded you? Be strong and courageous. Do not be terrified; do not be discouraged, for the LORD your God will be with you wherever you go" (Joshua 1:9).

Denis Waitley says in his "Inner Winner" audiotapes that we don't have to let other people rain on our parade. That doesn't mean we can control what happens to us, but we can control our reactions to people and circumstances.

Regardless of the nature of our problem, let's listen as God calls us by name and whispers His peace to us.

The Divine Presence

Continue to work out your salvation with fear and trembling (Philippians 2:12).

Have you ever attended a retreat which was so uplifting and inspiring that you came home knowing you'd never be the same again? But a few weeks later you were disappointed to find yourself back in the same old rut? Living in the same circumstances, you found yourself reacting much as you did before.

We've been told "the answer to every problem is a right relationship with God." That's right, of course, but we continually grow in our knowledge of the meaning and depth of that relationship. It takes time to work out our salvation and bring it to maturity.

Sometimes we may feel disappointed because we are unable to live on a perpetual mountaintop. But God accepts us where we are. He is working in us, and He wants us to accept ourselves as He does.

In his book *Jesus, Set Me Free*, George Maloney quotes from Romans 7 (Paul's "slave-to-sin" chapter) and then he says, "We have seen how Jesus comes to free us from such 'interior slavery.' This is, however, a constant process of turning within and letting the Divine Presence enter into the inner darkness with His freeing love."

Reverend Maloney explains it is not the outside forces that enslave us and cause problems, but those forces deep within us. How can we cooperate with God and "work out our salvation" which Paul admonishes us to do? We can learn to better understand ourselves and the reason we sometimes react in ways less than desirable. We have buried a great deal of information about ourselves below our level of consciousness.

If I react negatively to a person or situation, I may need to stop and ask myself why I got upset, or what I have within that triggered my reaction. Am I so insecure in my knowledge of who I am in Christ that I allowed this person or situation to disturb my peace?

Having discovered the source of my negative emotion, I can ask the Lord to break the chain of the emotion. It may be that the only way I can break the chain is to get a better sense of God's loving care for me. To get a deep sense of God's love requires that we spend time alone with Him and His Word. Paul spent three years alone in the desert before beginning his public ministry.

God is not as eager to get things done as He is that we develop a loving relationship with Him. The reason John was called the beloved disciple was that he was receptive to Jesus' love. He allowed the Lord to love him.

Minister and author Lloyd John Ogilvie says, "The Lord wants us to love ourselves as loved by Him and give ourselves the gift of time each day for stress-reducing communion with Him." With a similar thought, George Maloney says, "You can be that noble and beautiful child of so loving a Father. You can become, by His power, your true self."

We Never Fight Alone

Caleb silenced the people before Moses and said, "We should go up and take possession of the land, for we can certainly do it" (Numbers 13:30).

*Y*ou may recall the story of Moses sending out the twelve men to explore the land of Canaan which God had promised them. Ten of the men brought back a negative report, saying they could not possibly conquer the land because of the giants living there. When Caleb insisted they could succeed, they replied, "We seemed like grasshoppers in our own eyes, and we looked the same to them" (Numbers 13:33). Only two of the 12 recognized their God-given ability to conquer the giants in the land.

If we knew the truth, we also might find a small ratio of Christians today who feel capable of conquering their giants. As the Israelites needed to explore the geographical land, we may need to explore the land of our minds by asking ourselves a few questions: Is my heart inhabited with fear of what lies ahead? Do I have feelings that need God's healing touch? Are my dominant thoughts self-defeating,or are they conducive to spiritual and emotional growth?

Christian psychiatrist Paul Tournier said we have in the depth of our souls a secret closet whose key we have lost. Finding the key and inviting the Lord to enter that closet may be our first step toward conquering our giants.

The problem of the Israelites came not in their failing to explore the land thoroughly but in their thinking they'd have to conquer the land in their own strength. That's why they saw themselves as grasshoppers.

How often you and I may have seen ourselves as grasshoppers. Apart from the Holy Spirit, we are as powerless as grasshoppers against our spiritual enemies. But we're never left to fight our battles alone. God, who calls us His beloved children, never leaves us without support.

Whatever the nature of our giants, God will strengthen us and enable us to conquer them. The very circumstances which seem to be destroying us can become our friends. It isn't *what* happens to us but *how we handle* those happenings that's important. Stones that seem to block our path can become stepping-stones to victory.

One of our most frequently encountered giants is fear or anxiety. Psychologist Rollo May says anxiety is one of the most urgent problems of our day. Two other giants we often have to deal with are despair and discouragement. They show up from time to time on the turf most of us are on.

Discouragement is to be anticipated. Jesus warned that we would have tribulation. And Peter and James wrote that we are to expect trials. All such experiences may discourage us, but they need not defeat us.

In Gethsemane, Jesus was deeply distressed even though He knew God was in control. He was in despair but not defeated. You and I can expect times of despair, but we can know these times will pass. With God's help we can be conquerors of every spiritual giant we encounter.

Trusting God's Faithfulness and Mercy

I will sing of the mercies of the LORD forever; with my mouth will I make known Your faithfulness to all generations (Psalm 89:1 NKJV).

*T*o David, the Lord's mercies were so real that he determined to sing about them and make His faithfulness known to everyone. Moses, to whom Psalm 90 is attributed, expressed joy and satisfaction in knowing God's mercies: "Oh, satisfy us early with Your mercy, that we may rejoice and be glad all our days!" (Psalm 90:14 NKJV).

It sounds as if these two men were so well-acquainted with the mercies of God that nothing else mattered. They realized that whatever befell them, they could count on God's faithfulness to sustain them.

Most of us do not consistently recognize the faithfulness of God. Our feelings get in the way. When that happens, we tend to forget that God's mercies are based completely on who *He* is, not on who we are or what we are. God's mercies reach out to the most undeserving among us. God always looks at us through eyes of love.

The apostle Paul reminds us, "If we are faithless, he will remain faithful, for he cannot disown himself" (2 Timothy 2:13). For God to fail to be faithful to Himself would be for Him to be untrue to His own nature. God cares about everything that happens to us.

We may find it difficult to trust God when we see no evidence of His blessings. But we can *choose* to put our hope and trust in Him. Trust is a matter of choice, an act of the will. It does not depend on feelings. Feelings will eventually follow—after we have made the commitment to trust.

Trusting God's mercies begins with a knowledge of God's loving-kindness. As we read His inspired Word, we can note how He manifests His mercies. Then we can ask Him to make His words come alive to us and create faith in our hearts.

When we are in a situation in which we feel as if God's mercies are missing, it is helpful to tap into our past. We can recall a time when we felt God's loving presence. As we relive an experience when God's love was especially real to us, we can bask in that memory and then remind ourselves that "Jesus Christ is the same yesterday and today and forever" (Hebrews 13:8). What He once did, He can do again. He wants us to know we can trust the wideness of His mercy.

Fredrick W. Faber wrote a hymn, "There's a Wideness in God's Mercy," we can use to remind ourselves of God's mercy:

> There's a wideness in God's mercy,
> Like the wideness of the sea;
> There's a kindness in His justice,
> Which is more than liberty.
> If our love were but more simple,
> We should take Him at His Word,
> And our lives would be all sunshine
> In the sweetness of our Lord.

Sharing Blessings

*A word aptly spoken is like apples of gold
in settings of silver* (Proverbs 25:11).

*W*hen you feel in special need of a blessing, you
can be a blessing to someone else—and blessings will flow back to you. Your cheerful words
may be like a silver dish full of shining apples in
someone's drab day. If the woman at the checkout
counter seems unkind, she may be struggling with
a hurt. The sweetness of your smile may help allevi-
ate her pain. When people fail to respond to your
friendliness, it could be that they feel imprisoned in
loneliness. Your caring words may crack their prison
door.

Occasionally, when I receive a call from someone who is hurting, I send up a silent prayer, "Lord,
I don't feel like 'ministering' to anyone, but I'm

willing to be a channel of your healing love. Speak through me." He does, and my caller is blessed— and so am I.

When a friend calls or when I sit down to answer a letter, I sometimes remind myself of Isaiah's words:

> The Lord GOD has given Me
> The tongue of the learned,
> That I should know how to speak
> A word in season to him who is weary.
> —Isaiah 50:4 NKJV

Hurting people are not looking for advice, correction, theological lessons, or intellectual answers. They're looking for someone who cares, who understands, who can be trusted with their concerns— a person who accepts them without judgment. Regardless of our own weaknesses, you and I can be such persons.

We don't have to wait until all our wounds are healed before we become channels of God's healing love. We can, as Henri Nouwen says, make our "own wounds a source of healing" by a "constant willingness to see one's own pain and suffering as rising from the depth of the human condition which all men share." Daring to share our own weaknesses, we become one with our fellow sufferers. In so doing we bear each other's burdens (see Galatians 6:2).

These words from Isaiah apply to you and me: "Comfort, comfort my people, says your God. Speak tenderly . . ." (Isaiah 40:1,2). Although they may not verbalize it, almost everyone is in need of comfort and tender encouragement.

You have likely heard "sticks and stones can break my bones, but words can never hurt me." Don't believe it. Words have the power to heal or to hurt, according to the way we use them.

As we spend time alone with Jesus, He will affirm us and make us affirming persons. We can be a blessing to everyone we meet.

*Other Books by
Marie Shropshire*

In Touch with God

God Whispers in the Night

You're Never Alone

God Can Heal Your Broken Heart

*Yours to Love: Words of
Wisdom from Your New Baby*